ADVENTURE CARAVANNING WITH DOGS

YEAR 1 - FUR BABIES IN FRANCE

JACQUELINE MARY LAMBERT

Copyright & Disclaimer

From Wage Slaves to Living the Dream

Adventure Caravanning with Dogs

Year I – Fur Babies in France

Jacqueline Lambert

To Mark – My Soul Mate and the Man of my Dreams!

CONTENTS

PROLOGUE - DECEPTIVE BENDS

"I am not even going to look" I screamed as Mark hugged the caravan as far as he could into the high stone wall to our left and I hugged Kai, wrapping my fingers tightly in his fur. We had advanced our 40ft caravan / van combo cautiously into the narrow, blind corner at a snail's pace. This was fortunate, as we didn't see the oncoming wide load until it was too late. He hove into view as he swung recklessly around the corner at about forty miles-an-hour, half way across the centre line on the wrong side of the road.

We both closed our eyes and tensed. What could we do other than wait for the inevitable? It would be a near head-on impact. I was praying that Mark would survive; it wouldn't be so bad if we were at least both able to work out what to do once the entire right-hand side of the van and caravan had been ripped off.

To this day, neither of us knows how the truck missed us. It could only have been by millimetres. Yet the nature of the load carried by the oncoming HGV was the most ironic thing about the whole incident. It would have been typical of our luck but just too ridiculous to have been taken out by a static caravan!

It was our first day of Living the Dream.

We had gone from First-Timers to Full-Timers in only a month. We had accidentally bought a caravan and within a day (and a couple of bottles of CCC – Caravan Celebratory Champagne!) had made the perfectly sensible progression from having a couple of holidays in her each year to getting rid of everything that we owned, renting out our apartment and touring in her full-time to Live the Dream! After a practice run of a week, this near-miss with a static almost spelled a very early end to the Dream. We had been on tour for less than half an hour - and had made it only a couple of miles up the road from where we had collected our caravan.

D Day (Departure Day) had not gone to plan. Amid the frantic exit clean and final packing, we had been late getting away and by the time we had picked up the caravan, it was the height of the Friday evening rush hour. We had another near-miss on the motorway; a woman did an emergency stop directly in front of us to allow a lorry to merge from the slip road. Then, making the sharp turns required to get on to our site, we squared off our jockey wheel. (The jockey wheel is the small, retractable wheel at the front of the caravan.) Unsurprisingly, by the time that we had pitched, we were just a little bit tense!

We had arrived on site with no food or fundamentals like WINE. We really needed wine. We hadn't yet learnt to check ahead whether a site had EHU (electrical hook-ups) and shower blocks, so we were on a CL (Certified Location) in the middle of a field with no facilities and reliant on our solar panel for power.

We found a Chinese Takeaway nearby and just after dinner, which we finally ate at 10pm, we christened our pristine new shower with our four dogs. A little disconcerted by their change of circumstance, they had decided to add to the general air of relaxation by barking incessantly before all rolling in fox poo when they went out for their last pee. Lani had great clumps of it stuck to her collar. Fellow dog owners will agree that there are few smells more persistent and revolting than fox poo. The minty shower gel that we used to bathe our pooches did little more than disguise the stench.

So here we were, sitting a caravan that reeked of fox poo overlaid with mint shower gel and a hint of Chinese food. I was so tired and stressed after the trials of the day that I just wanted to cradle my head in my hands and weep uncontrollably.

It was not how I had expected to feel on our first day of Living the Dream!

INTRODUCTION

This book was written so that you can see where our desire to travel and experience life has taken us since the conventional world of work, eat and sleep ended abruptly in redundancy.

Pets, long hours and long commutes were not compatible, so when we both lost our jobs, satisfying a long desire to share our lives with a dog was our first indulgence. We intended to get two dogs, so that they could keep each other company, but accidentally ended up with four. We love them dearly and I named the book Adventure Caravanning with Dogs because where we go, our dogs go too.

The Adventure bit comes from our tendency to boldly go where no van has gone before... albeit not always fully intentionally!

We found it difficult to find information on travelling with dogs and are often asked "How DO you manage to travel with four dogs?!" It is surprisingly easy! With pet passports and the PETS travel scheme, quarantine is a thing of the past and travelling through most of the more mainstream EU countries doesn't even require you to stop at the border.

The other thing that people want to know is "How did you do it?" It seems that the lifestyle that we have chosen is what they always dreamed of – retiring early and seeing the world. This book should give you an idea of how we got there and also give some insight into how others whose paths we have crossed during our travels have managed to achieve their own ways of Living the Dream.

And since our other passions are windsurfing and skiing, you might find a bit about that too!

THE FIRST STEP: DISCOVERING THE PATH TO TRUE HAPPINESS!

"You Can't Sail to New Horizons Without Losing Sight of the Shore!"

It was through accident, not courage that I managed to lose sight of the shore. Other than meeting my second husband, Mark, it was one of the best things that ever happened to me!

In my 30th year, I moved to London on my own. Recently divorced, I was young, free, single – and was planning my first holiday on my own. I thought that a sailing or activity holiday might be more fun than sitting on a beach by myself. As a new girl about town, I needed to meet people and build a new life. I joined an activity club called Spice UK and tried lots of new things like tiger cuddling, fire eating and skydiving. So when my monthly Spice magazine flollopped onto my doormat and I turned a page to find "Rafting the Zambezi – River of the Gods" staring at me, I booked it straight away. I didn't even read the description!

I had never heard of white water rafting. It wasn't much of a "thing" in those days. My vision of the holiday was floating down this most iconic of African rivers on a wooden raft, looking at elephants, zebra and giraffes. Instead, the River of the Gods delivered colossal Grade 5 rapids (Grade 6 is unrunnable), 15-foot crocodiles, hippos (THE most dangerous animal in Africa) along with a fabulous diversity of tropical diseases.

However, this six day, 60km descent of the Zambezi between Victoria Falls and Kariba changed my life!

I slept under the stars each night on beaches beside the river. If I opened my eyes during the night, I saw the Southern Cross and the Milky Way swathed across the sky. With no light pollution to diminish their majesty, I could understand perfectly why ancient peoples used to worship the be-jewelled heavens. The secret stretch of the river that we ran was protected by the black, basalt cliffs of the Botoka Gorge, which towered hundreds of feet high on either side. The Botoka Gorge can be reached only via the raging waters of the mighty Zambezi. As such, it is a place as remote and inaccessible as the moon to most people. Somewhere between the privileged view of this natural beauty, the simplicity of owning only two sets of clothing (wet and dry) and the adrenaline of "serious down time" under some of the biggest white water in the world, I found that for me, the path to true happiness is in experience, not owning STUFF.

After such a "near life" experience, I found it difficult to adjust when I returned to civilisation and work. The daily grind just seemed so pointless. I wanted to escape. I wanted to be granted more than a two week annual window to see the world. I determined that I no longer wanted to live my life in thin slices.

"Can I have maternity leave?" I asked my boss. "What? You don't even have a boyfriend!" he scoffed. "Well, that's the beauty of it," I told him. "I am not going through all that messy business of childbirth. I just want a year off so that I can travel – then have my job back when I come home."

He was so taken aback that he said yes!

While I did have to come back, it was not all bad. Having vowed that marriage for a second time was a triumph of hope over experience, I met Mark at a Spice social function. We were engaged 37 days later. Then 37 weeks after meeting, we were married. We have been soul mates ever since and share the same aspirations – to really LIVE life and quit the rat race.

It was a long road and we were always planning. Sell up and buy a cheaper property in Italy. A B&B in Wales. A holiday cottage in the New Forest... We made changes to our circumstances to get more of what we wanted in life. We downsized our home and moved from London to the South Coast to enable us to live in the countryside, where we could do more windsurfing, walking and cycling. Many of the life plans were discarded, but eventually one will always come along that can be modified and moulded into a keeper.

But opportunity seldom comes laid out neatly and garnished on a plate. It would be nice to think that life would just allow you to win the Lottery, then go on and live your dreams, happy ever after in an eternal spring of sunshine and cornflakes, but unfortunately, life is not really like that.

We underwent the shattering experience of both losing our jobs and becoming too ill to work as a result. At the time, it was hard to see how this could be something posi-tive, but sometimes a really good, hard kick up the behind is the only way to force a change when things have got comfortable. Being told in your early fifties that you are no longer relevant after a lifetime of loyal service is certainly a tough one to come to terms with. Add to that the worry of how you will finance yourself into retirement and beyond in an unofficially ageist corporate world, while coping with the mental distress of the actual redundancy process, it was definitely not easy to view this as Opportunity Knocks!

We had long had that rolling 5-year plan that we would give up work and travel, but the truth is that it is hard to justify giving up a secure, well-paid job voluntarily. It is the golden handcuff; "If we work just one more year, we will have so much more security for the future!" We thought that we might set a deadline at age fifty five, but we never reached that. With the redundancy, the rolling plan just stopped dead in its tracks.

2

HOW TO ACCIDENTALLY BUY A CARAVAN – A CARAVAN CALLED KISMET STEP 1

From "Who could possibly want a caravan?" to Upper Class Trailer Trash!

"Why on EARTH would we want to come to The Motorhome and Caravan Show?!" was our shocked reaction to our friends' invitation to the NEC.

Our motor homing buddies Helen, Bernie and Steve took it well. Even with the inherent implication that a corned beef tin on wheels, with musty furnishings, uncomfortable beds and a potty, could be deemed a desirable holiday residence by anyone but a madman.

Then we all went on a camping holiday to Brittany in 2012. You remember 2012? The London Olympics? The Queen's Golden Jubilee? It rained. A lot. Luckily, Helen and Bernie were very generous with their motorhome, allowing us a much drier and more luxurious view of the rain. We sat in their awning, with lights, warmth and hot cups of tea. It was much better than our tent.

While in Brittany, we chatted to a few of the retirees who turn up in in their caravans and motorhomes every year to windsurf. Few had come from home. They spoke to us of international touring; of campsites where you could fall out of your mobile home onto a windsurfer; they caused the germ of an idea to form.

"Can we come with you to The Motorhome and Caravan Show?" we begged the following year.

Helen, Bernie and Steve took it well.

This was the start of our annual pilgrimage to The Caravan and Motorhome Show to scope out the motorhome of our dreams. One that would be available second-hand in a couple of years, when we were ready. One that could accommodate all of our windsurfers, bikes and Mark, who is 6'6" (2m) tall. None of them did – but that California Dream of following the sunset with a surfboard on your roof is a tough one to shake.

The rivalry between factions is never so bitter as that between those with strikingly similar interests. Skiers and snowboarders; windsurfers and kite surfers; but there is none more harsh than that between Motorhome and Caravan owners.

Add to that the fact that caravans are generally deemed to be a pain in the backside on the roads. Jeremy Clarkson expresses his hatred of caravans scientifically. He uses gravity – he pushes them off cliffs. Combustion – he uses explosives. Clarkson is not alone. It is a truth universally acknowledged. Caravans are just not cool.

Helen, Bernie and Steve took it well.

Motorhome owners all, they said that they would probably still speak to us if we bought a caravan. The awful realisation was dawning that the answer to our capacity and internal height problems was not an uber-cool motorhome, but a caravan towed by our toy box. By which I mean our trusty Hyundai iLoad van, Big Blue.

Arguments For a Caravan:

- **Cheap** – a new top-of-the-range caravan was approximately 1/3 of the purchase price of a new, basic motorhome. That translated into a couple of extra years that we didn't need to work to afford it.
- **Practical** – a 7.5m pantechnicon (one big enough for us to live in full-time) would not be suitable for nipping to the shops, sightseeing and, most importantly, would be unable to get kit to windsurfing beaches down narrow, winding lanes such as those found in Cornwall.
- **Economical** – a large motorhome was not really an option as our only means of transport. If we opted for a caravan, we already owned a suitable tow vehicle; our van Big Blue. That meant that we didn't need to buy another car and would need to tax, insure, fuel and maintain only one motor vehicle.
- **Sensible** – Why do large motor homes tow cars? Why not just tow a caravan?

Arguments Against a Caravan:

- "It's just not cool"

This was looking increasingly difficult to justify. While motorhomes are perfect for moving on regularly with minimal packing up or bagging a free night in a French Aire or pub car park, our plan was to pitch up, stay a while, see the sights and windsurf. A caravan? Really – it was a no-brainer.

"We're going to look at caravans at The Motorhome and Caravan Show..."

Helen, Bernie and Steve disowned us.

Thankfully, it was only for the day, as they were in the motorhome section at the NEC. We came back with a shortlist. It was quite short – a Bailey Unicorn Vigo was the caravan of our dreams. Mark could fit on the transverse bed and stand up everywhere. Even in the shower, which, at the time, we thought would be important!

A Caravan called Kismet – Step 2

If we hadn't gone to visit Steve in his motorhome, we would not have met the bloke with a Bailey caravan, who told us that the Bailey dealer was just around the corner.

If we hadn't decided go to Shepton Mallet instead of the Romsey Caravan Show to scope out the brand new Knaus Sportcaravan, we might not have decided to swing back via the Bailey dealer to see both the tiny Knaus and the opulent Bailey on the same day, by way of comparison.

If we hadn't gone via the dealer, I would not have spotted the 1-year-old Bailey Unicorn Vigo tucked around the back. She had come in the day before and smelled of two things; brand new and "bargain".

"That won't be here by the end of the weekend" said the salesman. It was a tactic, clearly, but I knew that there was truth in his statement. After a couple of coffees, a bit of soul searching (by Mark, not me) we had signed on the dotted line. Whatever the weather, there would be no tent for us in Brittany.

We named her 'Kismet', which means 'Fate'. And that, dear reader, is how we accidentally bought a caravan!

3

CARRY ON CARAVANNING PART 1 - 3 STEPS TO HEAVEN

Step 1 – The Accidental Purchase: 8th April

We had just 'gone to look' but had accidentally bought our 7.34m of caravan heaven. She is a 4-berth, so the dogs are sorted. We were not sure where we would sleep, however.

Step 2 – Some Sums: 9th April

Ooooh. My head. We were both suffering from CCS – Caravan Celebration Syndrome.

At some point last night, possibly some way down the second bottle of Caravan Celebratory Champagne, we had a "Eureka!" moment. Caravanning is a cheap way to live and after all, taking off and travelling is something that we had long been talking about.

It was a bit scary; thinking about stopping the talk and walking the walk – and starting the walk RIGHT NOW!!!! But we rationalised this;

If we were to travel permanently in the caravan and rented out our home, we would have no bills to pay and the rent would provide a small income. We had some savings and, with the rent coming in, it might be enough to tide us over until we reached the magic age of 55, at which point we could draw on our private pensions. If we ran short, there was always the option of a short-term or seasonal job to top us up.

At Christmas, many businesses take on extra staff. As a worst-case-scenario, three months' work over the Festive Season would still leave the summer free to travel. Other options would be consultancy or interim management, although having finally reached escape velocity from the corporate world, albeit not voluntarily, we were keen not to burn up on re-entry!

So how did we retire early?

We have been told so many times; "We would love to do what you are doing!" and asked "You look very young to be retired. How did you do it?" Here, I will tell you our little secret.

1. *If you want to retire at any time, never mind early, the first question you need to ask yourself is "How much money do I need to support the lifestyle that I want?"*

It has surprised me that not one single person who professes to want to live the life that we now do has even thought about this, never mind been able to answer the question!

We had been very diligent in keeping a detailed record of our expenditure for over a decade. If you don't know what you spend and what you spend it on, how can you know the minimum amount that you need to survive financially?

You also don't know where you can make savings. Like us, you probably pay no attention to the odd £2 that you spend here and there on a coffee, but we discovered that we were spending nearly £100 per month in Costa. That is almost £1200 per year, which equates to a few months of campsite fees. I dare you to add up what you spend on the little things that you barely notice. You will probably get a £BIG surprise!

Of course, the big unknown in retirement planning is how long you will live – and these days, you may be lucky enough to live beyond 100. You need to ensure that you have a sustainable source of income to last you for the rest of your life.

   1. *Unless you are minted, the next question you need to ask is "What are you prepared to forgo to live within your vastly reduced means?"*

Are you prepared to sacrifice big houses, posh cars, take-aways, fancy restaurants, expensive nights out, theatre trips, chic clothes, fab holidays, memberships, subscriptions, classy wines, upgrading your car or your tech every year – and the whole plethora of things that advertisers place before you to help you to squander your hard-earned cash?

If it meant that we would never have to work again, we found that we were prepared to sacrifice quite a lot of life's little luxuries!

You need to be realistic about the lifestyle you want. If, like us, you have been wage-slaves all your life and haven't won the Lottery, it is unlikely to be "Champagne Charlie", so you need to be sure that you can live with that and be happy.

However, we were fortunate in a couple of ways;

Firstly, as we worked hard and our careers blossomed, we didn't fall into the trap of living to our means with an ever more extravagant lifestyle. We had modest cars, rather than gas-guzzling status symbols. We saved hard and paid off our mortgage early. Then instead of spend, Spend, SPEND, we pretended that we still had a mortgage and salted all of that money away. Over the years, our assets accumulated so that they could provide a foundation income for our life without work.

Instead of buying a bigger house, we downsized and invested the capital in additional buy-to-let properties. We don't have children, so a one bedroom apartment was perfectly big enough for the two of us. It was cheap to run and with the hoover plugged into the lounge, I could vacuum the whole flat without even unplugging it.

I don't know about you, but I have never heard of anyone claiming on their deathbed that they wished they had spent more time doing housework!

Secondly, we are blessed that we enjoy the simple things in life – the outdoors, windsurfing, cycling and walking. We already had all the sports equipment that we needed for our hobbies, so most of our pleasures cost little or nothing. We still wanted to enjoy life – nobody wants to live like a pauper – so we budgeted to replace major items when necessary; our windsurfing kit, our van, Big Blue – and we could allow ourselves the occasional treat, like a meal out. We calculated that while wouldn't be rich, we would have ENOUGH – and ENOUGH is all you need.

And do you know, even when we were sober, it still sounded like it might just work out!

Step 3 – and...PANIC!!!!!!; The Rest of April

Wow! So much to sort out; we couldn't collect Caravan Kismet immediately, because she had to have her service and pre-delivery inspection. While we were massively excited, we persuaded the dealer to hang on to Kismet for as long as possible, to give us time to get prepared. We hadn't expected to be caravan owners, never mind permanent caravan dwellers. Our only vehicle, Big Blue, didn't even have a tow ball fitted!

The dealer kindly gave us a month. A caravan is a large item to store for free, so we really appreciated their patience. C Day (Collection Day) was set for the 10th May; before then, we had to pack up and rent out our home; sell unwanted possessions (i.e. most of them!) – and get to grips with a bewildering array of unexpected hurdles, most of which were acronyms that we didn't understand. We had to sort out:

1. Caravan Insurance – we had to deliver the weirdest information about the technical specs of our caravan, like whether the ALKO stabiliser is electronic or manual. What IS an ALKO stabiliser?
2. Then, what are VIN Chips, CRiS, ALKO locks and what is a CASSOA storage site? We needed a handle on all of these mysteries to arrange our insurance.
3. We also needed a tow ball, obviously, but single or twin? 7- or 13-pin?

The tow ball was a particular highlight for me. Owning a caravan was heady enough, but in my wildest dreams, I had never thought that one day, I would be the proud owner of a Fixed Flange Ball – with Electrics!

As you get to know me, you will find out that I love a double entendre. You will come to realise that I had no choice but to slip that one in.

Luck = Planning + Opportunity

People often tell us how lucky we are and I absolutely

agree. But what they don't always appreciate is that getting this lucky didn't just drop in our lap – it did involve quite a bit of work!

We were certainly lucky that the opportunity came along. As for spotting that both of us losing well-paid jobs, suddenly and simultaneously was an opportunity, rather than "Game Over" – then grabbing that opportunity and making it work; well that was down to us.

The luckiest people that we know are the ones who work hard and make brave but calculated decisions. This "opportunity" was something that we had been seeking and planning for over ten years, so when it came along, albeit unexpectedly and with appallingly bad timing, we were ready. It did not pass us by.

So those are our Three Steps to Caravan Heaven and Living the Dream without working. If it is something to which you aspire, there is no time like the present to start planning.

Most people do not spend even half as much time planning their personal lives as they do planning their careers. If they did, they would be unstoppable.

So if you want to Live the Dream, off you go and make yourself some luck!

4

CARRY ON CARAVANNING – PART 2: THE MAIDEN VOYAGE

"All the Gear and No Idea!" Our first ever caravan experience!

It was C Day. Caravan Collection Day and today, the early heatwave that had made the news miraculously exchanged itself for a Severe Weather Warning. I can't tell you how delighted we were to have been blessed with such perfect "Introduction to Caravanning" weather!

The dealer gave us a two-and-a-half hour introductory lecture on the features of our new caravan. We received detailed advice on putting up and collapsing the folding table and how to remove the microwave plate for travel. Well that's the bit I remember. Then they hitched us up and sent us on our way, notepad full and minds reeling with corner steadies, Whale pumps, Alde heaters, Aquarolls, CALOR cylinders, Wastemasters, hitch and wheel locks, towing mirrors, gas fridges, scary cassette toilets and when to use Elsan blue, pink and green fluid, but just a quick skim over hitching, unhitching and all those funny bits at the front.

Our first journey was an epic. We travelled approximately 1.5 miles. "That's a nice van! Been caravanning long?" was our greeting from one of the wardens, Steve, as we arrived on site. "Our first day..." we muttered sheepishly. Steve gave us the grin of a man who had seen it all before. "Do you have a motor mover?" "Er. No. Mark is very confident in his reversing..." Nevertheless, it was with genuine warmth that Steve said "I'll try and put you on a fairly level pitch. Follow me."

That we were "All The Gear and No Idea" became evident immediately. We couldn't even unhitch the caravan! "Are you having trouble?" asked a pleasant chap called Granville, who wandered over having spotted that we'd been fiddling about with our tow hitch for about half an hour.

Granville soon had us sorted. "Pop on the caravan handbrake and just pull your tow car forward a couple of inches" he said.

The reason that we couldn't unhitch was because we were suffering from a compressed tow hitch.

Although Steve had kindly found us a pitch that we could drive straight on to with no manoeuvring, we had reversed to line up the hole for the ALKO wheel lock, which has to be EXACTLY in the middle of the gap in the alloys. It was lucky that we couldn't unhitch; if we had, Granville told us that the compressed tow hitch would probably have shot forward as it de-compressed and punched a dent in Big Blue's backside!

We managed to set up almost level, attach the hitch and wheel locks, then get the water, waste and electricity connected. It only took us five hours! We sat back with a frothy cuppa (we hadn't purged the water system) and rather enjoyed the relaxing thunder of torrential rain hammering down on our Alu-tec roof. Certainly, it was preferable to the sound of torrential rain on canvas, which, come to think of it, has accompanied our EVERY other camping experience!

After two days, our perfect 'Introduction to Caravanning' weather continued with a lightning storm at 13:00. "We're OK" I reassured Mark. "The caravan will act as a Faraday Cage and protect us from the lightning."

It cleared a bit later, so Mark decided to tackle The Awning. We had specified the awning very carefully – we just asked the dealer for "The biggest one" and oh my – this one came complete with its own Double Entendre. It was HUGE!

I was a bit scared of the awning – and with good reason. My caravanning cousin warned that divorce proceedings have frequently been initiated over an awning. However, I can share with you now the perfect 'No Tears' approach to putting up an awning. I supervised from a chair, having a cup of tea with my friend Helen, because the sight of a brand-new awning on the ground was like honey to a bee; it attracted every bloke on the site. They all wandered over to rub their chins with Mark and help him to organise his poles. Helen and I regarded them happily from the comfort of our now sun-bathed deck chairs and christened them 'The Erection Section.'

Our motor homing friend Steve came midweek to join us on site, with his brother, Steve. I mean Andrew. Excuse me, but they are twins. It was like having Steve in stereo! Steve is a trailblazer of trailers; a Titan of towing; caravans, motorhomes, boats, portaloos (yes really!)   Steve is the Martini of reverse towing – any time, any place, anywhere, he can get it in. Ooer missus. (Sorry, but I did warn you about the Double Entendres.)

It was a relief to have some experienced brains to pick.

We had questions to ask about caravanning – and we didn't even know what they were.

As the week ended and our caravanning experiment came to an end, I took the Canine Crew for their last run through the buttercups on the ramparts of the Iron Age fort at Old Sarum while Mark packed up. I saw him do it. Then I saw him do it again. I ran over in panic; I was greeted with a perfect, wet cow pat defaced by two Kai-sized trenches straight through the middle. I walked back to the site unable to contain my laughter. Kai ran on ahead happily, straight through a newly-mown sports field, unconcerned that most of it adhered really nicely to the wet cow pat, which now covered most of his body.

"What cute dogs!" At the gate, an American lady leaned down to stroke Kai his full length. She recoiled in horror as her fingers met with soft fur, encrusted with a mixture of wet and drying cow pat, embedded with grass clippings that were hardening into a texture that resembled iron filings.

Mark had already disconnected the water from the caravan and the showers on site had a very insistent 'No Dogs' sign on them. We would not use the facilities to cleanse a cow-pat covered Cavapoo but there was no hose either. There was nothing for it. Puppy Love Is – crispy, green, cow-pat boy on your lap all the way to Selsey, which was where the caravan was going into storage. At least it took my mind off the terror of knowing that there was now a 1.5 tonne, 7.35m caravan following us all the way there. My heart was in my mouth for every, single one of the 62 miles.

Caravan storage – The Myth. I imagined that it was just like airport parking. Drop off the caravan; they pop it away for you. Ring up when you need it and arrive to find it valeted, ready and waiting for you to just hitch up and go.

Caravan storage – The Reality. Turn up at windswept,

deserted, gravel yard, traumatised after first real experience of towing; try to find a way to reverse into a space approximately 1mm wider than your large caravan. Find that there is not enough manoeuvring room in front of the space to accommodate your 40ft rig. (We did not yet know that it is not only possible – but much easier – to push the caravan around by hand on level ground!) Want to cry. Husband – confident in reversing skills – sticks it in, wiggles it about a bit and gets it right first time. Feel very proud – and almost faint with joy to have delivered an undamaged caravan safely into storage! Stop feeling sick with nerves and discover that you are STARVING. Take cow pat covered dog to café with outdoor seating area and try to conceal him and his singular aroma in a corner. Have all-day breakfast at 3pm. Sigh with relief.

I am not sure that we could class ourselves as real caravanners yet, but we had certainly been blooded!

5

LIVIN' THE DREAM WEEK 1 – HARE FARM, TWYFORD

Fox Poo, Ticks & Goose Eggs; a Caravan Manoeuvring Course – & a Near Death Experience!

5th June - It was D Day (Departure Day) minus 1. Packing up your entire life takes longer than you think. My hot tip here is to keep the pressure off yourself by NOT diverting from the main event by needing to post all the items you sold on eBay the night before you move permanently from 'The Brick' into a caravan.

Kai helped our efforts tremendously by starting to eat our environmentally friendly packing chips. So besides trying to clean the house, get all remaining worldly goods to fit inside the van and frenetically packaging oddly-shaped parcels at 10pm (how *do* you pack up a golf club for posting?) we were also soaking half-dissolved corn chips out of Kai's whiskers.

6th June - D Day. We were now Upper Class Trailer Trash and home would be where we parked it. All the essentials to see us through our travels were rammed into the van. We had one box of clothes each. The rest was either sports stuff or dog stuff. (By midweek in our first week, we took at least 1/3 of these "essentials" to store in Mark's Mum's loft! We have been shedding "essentials" ever since – two years into our touring, Big Blue now travels only half full.)

OUR FIRST DAY of Living the Dream did not go to plan. Indeed, it almost ended in tragedy half an hour after it started with a near-death experience. As I mentioned in the Prologue, we almost had a head-on collision with a static caravan! We had also damaged our jockey wheel - which would be the first of many breakages - and then found ourselves stranded in a field with no electricity, no food, no facilities and four dogs who had rolled in fox poo. Most importantly, we had no alcohol with which to console ourselves. It was not quite the carefree idyll that we had imagined!

HOWEVER, things always look better in the morning. We awoke to the sound of skylarks and watched swallows swoop and dive above a hare in the field. Our nearest neighbours were goats, alpaca and rare breeds of chicken. We had no electric hook-up, so our phones, computer and all connection with the outside world gradually ran out of charge and we finally found what we had been seeking. Peace!

Chewbacca, the billy goat kid had been born the day we arrived. He was feeding from only one side of his mum, Leia's udder. I had a part to play in remedying this. I used to look after some goats on a small holding during my summer holidays when I was a teenager. I was awarded two goose eggs for showing his owner Ruth how to milk Leia. Mark and I used my prize to cook the ULTIMATE fry up, served on our Wedgewood caravan plates, of course. We are Upper Class Trailer Trash, after all!

(Transporting our everyday china in the van while we were packing up our belongings, Mark had smashed the lot! The back door had flown open on a roundabout and our whole dinner service had fallen out onto the road. The only plates that we had left were part of our 'best' Wedgewood dinner service, which is what we still use to dine from in the caravan.)

We were sweltering in a mini heatwave and trimmed the dogs. We had bought them a paddling pool to help them cool off, but they seemed to think that it was just an over-sized drinking bowl! Then, of course, it turned cool and wet – just in time for me to spend the whole weekend outdoors doing my Caravan Manoeuvring course.

With the wet, warm weather and all the livestock around, the pups had a plague of ticks. We had to remove several each day. Poor Ruby had one on her eyelid and we had to take Kai to the vet to have the head of one tick taken out and a follow-up antibiotic injection administered.

The Woman at the Wheel – Practical Caravanning Course

Mark has an LGVI licence, which means that he is qualified to drive an articulated lorry. Other than a quick taster session at the Motorhome and Caravan Show, I had never towed anything before, so I signed myself up to a two-day Practical Caravanning Course. The truth is - I was absolutely dreading it.

The combined length of our caravan / van combo is 40-feet, which is similar in length to an artic. Many women leave towing to their husbands, but I felt that it was essential for me to be able to take the wheel. It would mean that we could share driving on long journeys but most importantly, we would not be stuck if some catastrophe befell Mark and meant that he was unable to drive. Mark's LGV Licence and my undertaking the course would also give us a discount on our insurance.

I shambled tentatively into a stark lecture room at Sparsholt College, eyes down as I grabbed myself a coffee and shuffled uncomfortably into a spare seat. I tried my best to be invisible but a U-shaped table was surrounded by unfamiliar faces, all of whom were staring blankly at me. Little did I know that they were all just as nervous as me!

As I plucked up the courage to look up and meet the staring eyes, I got a huge smile. The huge smile belonged to Bella. I found out later that she was 80-years old and wanted to learn to tow so that she could take the small caravan that she had bought at this year's Romsey Caravan Show up to the West Coast of Scotland.

It was a trip that she and her late husband had been planning to do. I pointed out to her that we almost had matching caravans. Mark and I HAD been going to the same show as her at Romsey but switched to Shepton Mallet at the last minute to view the Knaus Sportcaravan and compare it with the Bailey Unicorn Vigo. Bella had bought her caravan on the same day that we had accidentally bought our Bailey, Kismet. We were Caravan Twins!

Our instructors, Richard and Dave were lovely and as we went around the table doing introductions, I was heartened that not only were six of the twelve delegates ladies, but zero out of twelve of us had any towing experience whatsoever.

I really enjoyed the course and it cast some valuable rays of light on the whole mystery of caravanning; not just towing but things like Reverse Polarity on caravan electrics, which up until now, I had thought was something fictional to do with the cult musical "Return to the Forbidden Planet."

Reverse Polarity is not something that you will come across in the UK, however it is not uncommon in Europe. It occurs when the neutral or earth and live connections in the electrical hook-up are reversed. The problem with Reverse Polarity is that it allows electricity to flow even when an appliance is switched off, presenting a safety hazard. A socket tester will tell you immediately if you have Reverse Polarity and an adapter will correct it. Both are cheap and readily available. We bought ours from eBay but you will probably find them in caravan and camping shops.

Everyone was really encouraging and supportive – and we all passed with flying colours and got our certificates. Caravans were provided, but we were using our own tow vehicles, so we got plenty of practice hitching and unhitching. By the end, I could hitch and unhitch in my sleep! Having learnt hacks to help plan a line to drive through and reverse around an obstacle course, I felt much more confident about the idea of towing Kismet. "Manoeuvring a large caravan is much easier than manoeuvring a small one." Richard informed me. Well, we would see!

It is easier for a camel to pass through the eye of a needle than it is for Mark to...

I was Certified! I rang to tell my Dad. "It's about time..." he said.

I got back to the caravan and asked Mark what he had been doing while I had been on my course. He looked a bit sheepish and guilty. It took some time for him to admit to the occurrence of a Magic Markie Moment. He explained to me how he had spent most of the afternoon; "I was stuck in the caravan toilet..."

It appeared that after he had slid the bathroom door shut, a box had toppled over and wedged itself behind the sliding door on the outside and jammed it, so he was penned in the privy!

"How on earth did you get out?" I asked. "I climbed

out of the window..." I was incredulous. Quite how someone who is 6'6" tall could have clambered out of a window less than a foot high defeated me. He said that even he had been prone to doubts, but since I was out for the day and the dogs were getting agitated, he had no choice. Staggeringly, he had even managed to do it without breaking anything. He had recovered from his ordeal by treating himself to a Terry's Chocolate Orange lunch.

Since he had 'fessed up, at least I felt empowered to admit to my own particular brand of stupidity. I had set our new Snooper Caravan Sat Nav to get me back to the caravan from my course but couldn't understand why the road layout and instructions from the Sat Nav bore no resemblance to the route that I was actually driving. "I'm not going over a roundabout." I was thinking. "There is no side road here..." In fact, "Where the heck am I? This isn't the way I came!" I drove aimlessly around Hampshire for ages until I found something familiar. The Sat Nav was absolutely no help at all.

When the Sat Nav indicated The Hockley Interchange on the M3, the penny dropped. The map needed updating. I know the Hockley Interchange well. I had lived in Southampton many years ago and queued at the Hockley lights for forty minutes every morning and the same every evening on my long commutes to work. But that was twenty years ago, before the M3 extension was built (and before Sat Navs were invented...) The only explanation was that Sat Nav was clearly WELL out of date.

It was only when the Sat Nav showed me reaching my destination when I was still three miles away that I realised my mishtayke. I had pressed 'Go' on "Route Simulation" – so it was just scrolling through to show me the route that I had planned. With a combination of towering intellects like Mark's and my own, we would clearly go far!

As we departed from Hare Farm, Ruth thanked me for at least the 1000th time for helping her to milk the goat and Trevor guided us out past all the obstacles. After my course and with Trevor's help, I had managed to retract our damaged jockey wheel fully, which prevented it from catching again in the same place on the way out.

But we hadn't done too badly. Caravan Confucius Say – "Real knowledge is to know the extent of one's ignorance." In that sense, we were certainly beginning to become a little wiser.

We hit the road in the direction of Portland, where we were hoping to score some windsurfing. As it was, we had storms in store, a sunken road and a COLOSSAL sense of humour failure!

I am delighted to report that Bella did do her trip to Scotland – and was humbled by how friendly and helpful fellow caravanners were.

6

"YOU CAN'T READ THAT IN A BOOK!" – PEBBLE BANK, PORTLAND

"Trying is the first step towards failure." – Homer Simpson

I was still finding packing up and towing very stressful. My heart was in my mouth for the whole time that we spent on the road, but we did arrive at Portland unscathed. We had a tricky moment as we pulled into a wrong turning for reception at the Pebble Bank Campsite. We had to reverse out down a small incline to get back on to the road. Our jockey wheel, which we had squared off nicely at our last site, was just millimetres away from a further shave along the tarmac!

Pitching didn't get any less stressful. As trailer trash, we had one of the best seats in the house, with a perfect unobscured view of The Fleet, Chesil Beach and Portland. We even had beautiful barn owl hunting over the field directly in front of us. All this came at a cost, however.

Our caravanning learning curve had been a steep one and progressed basically as we broke things. The problem with siting the van here was that we couldn't tow her onto the pitch. We had elected not to have a motor mover; a decision made because they are expensive, drain the battery and reduce the already limited payload of the caravan. And Mark was confident in his reversing...

So here, we had no choice but to move the caravan by hand on our now-square jockey wheel; the first item that we had broken. Mark seemed to find letting the caravan run freely downhill towards a sheer drop exhilarating. "Put the brake on. PUT THE BRAKE ON!!!!!" I yelled as he cackled like a madman. I suffered a complete sense of humour failure as our only home, 1.5 Tonnes of caravan, was bearing down on me and heading for a 12-foot drop into a sunken lane.

Then came the levelling. I was feeling quite positive about the levelling. The instructor on my recent Caravan Course had given me an app for my phone. How could we fail?

The fly in the ointment (there is always one) was that because we had no understanding of things like electrical hook-up, we had accidentally been completely off grid for the whole of the previous week at Hare Farm. As such, the phone battery was completely dead. So the levelling process went thus; plug in the phone to charge sufficiently to load the app and then keep plugging it in between levelling readings so that it would always have *just* enough juice to take the next reading.

Like the Spirit Level app that we had tried on Mark's phone, which had left us with a pronounced list to port, it didn't work - but much more spectacularly! The levelling app maintained that we were still down at the front when we had raised the caravan to a position so vertical that she had assumed the attitude of an Apollo moon rocket on the launch pad, armed and ready for take-off. This extreme position broke off the foot on one of our back corner steadies. We fixed the corner steady by improvising with a tent peg. Then I levelled the caravan to perfection by rolling a tennis ball down the middle of the floor. You can't read THAT in a book.

No wonder that they told us on my Practical Caravanning course that "Caravanning is a spectator sport." Thankfully, we had turned up on site in the middle of the day, so I doubt that any entertainment was derived from this particularly spectacular show of incompetence.

The weather was mixed and entirely contrary to the forecast. On Tuesday, we had decided not to windsurf as there was a lot of rain due. In fact, it was beautiful sunshine and blowing a steady Force 5 westerly – a classic windsurfing day at Portland! In the end, we wouldn't have sailed anyway, since our Scottish friends, Renny and Katharine dropped in to visit from their tour of the South coast. Renny tested our levelling with his own app. My tennis ball approach had achieved a level within 1% of perfection. I felt quite smug!

Nevertheless, here we were caravanning. Another Severe Weather Warning had been issued. Tipton was under water.

We had a lot of visitors that week. I think that our friends couldn't quite believe that we really had gone and done it – rented out our apartment to live in the caravan. They all wanted to come and see for themselves.

People frequently ask us what we do with our time, now that we are not working. We seemed to be really busy. For example, Day 10 I spent lining my drawers with Anti-Slip. Livin' the Dream, people. Livin' the Dream!

On Sunday, it THREW it down all day. Helen and Bernie came to visit, very optimistically bringing bikes, windsurfing gear and a willingness to walk. We were confined to barracks and the highlight of the day was watching the dogs mesmerised by the screen saver on the TV! We put on a film and learnt another Caravan Confucius: "Many people drinking many cups of tea soon fill up chemical toilet." We had to take it out in the rain to empty it twice!

Then we had to think about leaving. We needed to push the caravan uphill off a wet, grass pitch on a square jockey wheel and try to hitch without being crushed to death or losing the caravan down the bank into the sunken lane. It's the sort of thing that could give one a sleepless night.

We also had potentially misplaced confidence in our ability to fashion a nose-weight gauge from some cheap bathroom scales and a broom handle, saving ourselves £40. We did read that in a book, but watch this space as to how we got on and whether the scales made it once they had a 1.5 tonne caravan on top of them!

The Ca-Lamberti Count from just over a week of touring amounted to; 1 Jockey Wheel Squared; 1 Corner Steady Pin Sheared; 4 Fridge Shelves Destroyed & Superglued back together. I haven't included the near-death experience here, since that only resulted in mental trauma. There was no actual damage.

I saw all this as EFT (Effective Failure Testing). I was uncomfortably aware, however, that our form so far did not bode well for our move off the pitch the following day.

I can confirm that all of these things did indeed give us a sleepless night. It was Midsummer Day; it had rained solidly for 36 hours; the caravan was rocking – and we had to get ready to roll!

Mark had needed to get up in the middle of the night to tighten up the improvised storm straps that were holding down the awning (fabricated from cam straps and dog tethers. You can't read THAT in a book) and open a vent in the awning to stop it from actually blowing away. The winds were consistently blasting a lusty Force 7 (near gale) and gusting Force 8 (gale). We considered ringing Bernie to see if he fancied going windsurfing now.

Don't you just dread Monday Mornings? However a bad day caravanning is better than a good day in the office and in the end, getting off the pitch proved unexpectedly straightforward. We simply swivelled Kismet around on the spot and hitched her up. All that worry was for nothing. It was as easy as that!

What was not so good was that all of our shoes (every pair that we own!) were sitting in a large puddle in the awning where the rain had blown through the open vent. We got the Yawning Awning down in the near gale and the kind of rain that you could only replicate by standing underneath Victoria Falls. It was teamwork! There was not so much as an urgent barked order and the mood remained positive even when I laughed heartily as cold water coursed off the awning roof and straight down Mark's neck.

The plan was to head over to the New Forest. This would be our last stop before we stepped off the edge of the known world and into that great caravanning chasm; The Continent.

7

THE GREAT CONTINENTAL DIVIDE

*Post-Brexit Europe; Our 4th Week Caravanning; Our 3rd Severe
Weather Warning; Pups in PRISON - & A Pitching Debacle.*

In preparation for stepping off the edge of the known world
(i.e. catching the ferry from Portsmouth to France for three
months) and some pre-departure root canal work, we had
moved from Portland to the New Forest Centenary Site.

Not only that, we did it IN THE SUNSHINE, with no
breakages or near-death experiences. In fact, we pitched so
seamlessly that we had time for a relaxing, post-arrival cup
of tea with home-made lime drizzle cake, replete with fresh
raspberries and blueberries. We felt like we were finally
getting the hang of this caravanning lark. It was most
pleasing.

Of course, it did mean that everything was going far too
swimmingly...so we were not in the least bit shocked when,
in our fourth week of caravanning, we got our third Severe
Weather Warning. A month's worth of rain fell on parts of
South East England and there were 1000 lightning strikes
per hour! The pups experienced their first real thunder-

storm. It prompted a bit of a bark-fest but they seemed to cope quite well.

Some Great Wit once said disparagingly "Camping and caravanning is a holiday that reproduces conditions found in refugee camps the world over!" I guess he had a partial point. Also renowned for its mud, sweat and beers, it was the weekend of the Glastonbury Festival. Really we should have known. Even before the band list was announced, severe weather was pre-ordained.

We were on a budget and this particular pitch was nice and flat. A perfect location for checking our nose-weight. You may remember that we had set ourselves the task of saving ourselves £40 on the purchase of a nose-weight gauge by fashioning our own from a set of cheap bathroom scales (£1.50 in Home Bargains) and a couple of bits of wood that we had foraged.

It is fair to say that there were those in our circle who expressed a slight lack of confidence in this approach. Some, indeed, articulated a complete desolation of faith in the remotest potential for a successful outcome. A few might even have gone as far as vocalising the word "Idiots..." But I am delighted to report that it worked BRILLIANTLY - and our nose weight came in at a perfect 70% of spec. So "Yah boo sucks to you." You unbelievers!

23rd June - It had happened. We went windsurfing with Helen for the last time on UK waters but only to take our minds off the Brexit referendum result. It was strange being on our "home beach" when we were actually now homeless – and Britain had voted to cast herself adrift from our destination, Europe. We got a gritty reminder of everything that we had forgotten about beach walks with the dogs; the caravan was soon filled with sand and the bed felt like we were sleeping on an emery board.

Thankfully, we had bought our Euros just before the pound plummeted to its 30-year low following the Brexit referendum result. Some currency dealers actually suspended trading; our friend Elaine couldn't buy even one, lonely little Euro to spend on her holiday the following week.

24th June – After a bit of a panic packing up and begging special dispensation for a late-departure from the campsite, we boarded our ferry at Portsmouth for the overnight crossing to St Malo. We settled in the bar with a beer and a bag of nuts. The ferry seemed very slow to get going. Following the UK's exit from the EU, Mark wondered aloud "Are we really under way, or is the ferry just tied to France and someone is slowly towing Britain further away from Europe?" On the ferry, we watched England lose to Iceland in the European Cup... Ahem. A second British exit from Europe in a week!

The following morning, we sat for some time over breakfast looking out at the port of St Malo. "Disembarkation will take a long time due to Action Industrielle" came the announcement. Well it was a Tuesday. Why would the French not be on strike? Britain out of Europe last week, last night – and then this morning, we found Europe doing its level best to keep us out!

We had booked kennels for our Fur Family on the ferry, thinking that it would be more comfortable for them during the crossing. They had to remain in the car after boarding, then, once the ship was under way, we returned with a member of staff to transfer them into the kennels.

It could not have been more awful. I just wanted to cry as we left them staring after us through the bars of their prison. I mean the kennel.

The hold of the ship was like hell. It reminded me of the set of the film 'Alien'. The kennels were in a corner of the deck right next to the huge, thundering engines. The deck itself was a stroboscopic cacophony of car alarms blaring and flashing all around us. The deafening racket was amplified to pain level as it echoed around the cavernous, metallic interior. Mark and I couldn't hear each other speak as we carried bedding and water bowls to the kennels. The stench of diesel from the engines made us feel sick. Our darling little puppy dogs followed us trustingly if cautiously, tails between their legs.

Dogs' sense of smell and hearing is much keener than ours, so it must have been even worse for them. Even poor Rosie, usually the bravest and boldest, was literally shaking with fear as we put her inside the kennel. They were supposed to be muzzled. The check-in lady gave us a muzzle; we tried it on our little Ruby, who just looked up at us with huge, sad eyes, as if to say "But I'd never do anyone any harm." It was horrible. I suppose that muzzles are a sensible precaution; the conditions down there were enough to turn the most docile family pet into a throat-tearing Hound of the Baskervilles. We could visit our babies at 10pm. I couldn't get over the haunted look in their eyes when we went back to see them. "What have you DONE to us?" they seemed to say.

We couldn't sleep knowing that our poor little lovelies would be scared and alone. We were ready and waiting half an hour early for the morning visiting time at 8am. The ten hour duration of the crossing was the longest that we have ever been apart from them! We'd had no morning cuddles and no little Ruby song to wake us up, just nightmares about dogs dying of cold, fear or overheating on ferries. The biggest irony was that it was Mark and I's first night without "the kids" since they had come into our lives – and we had been in bunk beds!

We had a very civilised brekkie in the restaurant on the ferry. Our final British fry up was presented to us under an elegant silver dome. Then, at last, it was time to get our beloved puppy dogs back. A well-meaning, but particularly loud and enthusiastic Scandinavian lady took a real shine to the fur babies. She was short and stout with bright orange hair. She was sporting a thick, hairy, lime-green mohair suit that seemed to enhance her width. As Ruby snuggled into my arms, happy to be delivered from hell and re-united with her human family, the lady came over to pet her; "SHEEEE'S A BAY-BEE!" she yelled delightedly. "A BAY-BEE!" She thumped Ruby affectionately over the head a couple of times. Boink, boink, boink. "SHE'S A BAY-BEE!!!"

Order was restored; we were all back together in Big Blue. As we disembarked from the ferry, some French dock workers handed us a leaflet complaining about their lot – that they only get 30-weeks' annual leave or something. We hit the RIGHT side of the road, "SHE'S A BAY-BEE" still ringing in our ears. The pups were shattered. Like us, I don't think they had slept a wink during the crossing.

The journey to our first stop in Penthièvre was uneventful. We got a spectacular view of Mont St Michel as we skirted the coast of Brittany, drove the van through Vannes (which I always find pleasing!) and arrived at Camping Municipal Penthièvre in warm sunshine. We got a pitch just one back from the sea for €16.50 per night with enhanced electricity. Enhanced, but not sufficient to power the microwave and *anything else* simultaneously!

We had a Magic Markie Moment. I think Mark got confused over the "Road" in the title of our "Road Refresher" – the new, non-splash travel dog bowl that we had bought for the trip. He forgot that he had left it on the ground while we were pitching Kismet and managed to carry out a Professor Denzel Dexter-style experiment; "Can this ordinary, plastic, dogs' drinking bowl withstand being driven over by a 3.5 tonne van?" The answer, surprisingly, was "Yes!"

For anyone watching us pitch the caravan, we gave a virtuoso performance. We lined up and reversed the caravan masterfully straight on to the edge of the pitch, but we had forgotten to leave room to park the van alongside. So we pulled off, lined up the caravan again, reversed into the perfect position in the middle and unhitched; but we had forgotten to level. Rather than going through the faff of hitching up again, we decided on another experiment "Is it possible to pull 1.5 tonne of caravan up a levelling ramp by hand?" Unsurprisingly, the answer to that one was "No…!"

So we re-hitched and pulled the caravan up the ramp with the van – and found that we were level. Hurrah! But we had forgotten to put on the ALKO wheel lock… So we jacked up the caravan to line up the holes for the lock, but when we let the jack down, the caravan was not level, so we jacked it up and down to move the levelling ramp, it was not level… and so it went on. Our efforts were not aided by the fact that the 3-way industrial sprit level that we had purchased at great expense to replace the levelling apps and the tennis ball gave different readings, depending on which way round we turned it.

We provided at least a couple of hours' entertainment to delight our little crowd of clandestine observers. It fully corroborated the advice from my Practical Caravanning Course; caravanning is definitely a spectator sport!

Mary and Keith, a couple of our windsurfing buddies wandered over to say hello. They are seasoned motor homers who have been touring Europe for decades. They are in no small part responsible for our current choice of lifestyle. Back in 2012, they were among those who had regaled us with stories of campsites where you could fall out of your mobile home straight onto your windsurfer, thus causing that germ of a lifestyle idea to form...

My absolute favourite approach to levelling, which I witnessed a few days later on site, was someone who had dug a deep trench straight through the pitch to accommodate their offside caravan wheel! We didn't have to resort to such extreme measures. After explaining the issue of our self-contradicting spirit level, Mary and Keith gave us the full benefit of their many years' experience regarding the mystery of levelling. "We check that the van is level by putting a glass of wine on the worktop." Now that sounds like the kind of proper plan GUARANTEED to prevent poor performance!

Pitching debacle over, we took the doggies for a run on the beach; a magnificent crescent of sand headed by Carnac, with the 10-mile peninsula of Quiberon curling gently round to cradle the southern end of the glistening, sapphire-blue bay.

By now, The Fab Four had forgiven us for the ferry. We did promise them faithfully that we would never put them through anything like that again. We would give them the run of the caravan on any future ferry crossings or we would take The Channel Tunnel, so that we could all stay in the van together.

They seemed to like France even better than their home town, Bournemouth. Ruby was frantically doing her job, running along the shoreline and sniffing madly while everyone else was jumping through pools, digging and chasing. It was lovely to see – a seamless transformation into Continental Cavapoos!

We were glad that they had settled in so well. Penthièvre was going to be home for a couple of weeks. Quite how many weeks it would be, we didn't realise at the time...

8

A POSTCARD FROM PENTHIÈVRE - PART 1

Blighted by Breakages, Technology & French Fusion Cuisine; A Trip To The Vet; THE Most Expensive Fish in the World - & A Road Trip to Nowhere!

It would be hard not to fall in love with the area around Penthièvre – shady, pine-scented woods; lanes fragranced with honeysuckle; chocolate–box villages of stone cottages, surrounded by hydrangeas and hollyhocks and a Neolithic stone monument at every turn.

And what about our first view of Quiberon bay? Two steps from our caravan were mirror-flat waters, like a jewel-blue infinity pool, fringed by a dramatic, sweeping arc of white sand. Carnac to the left and Quiberon, at the far end of the peninsula, were like mystical, golden cities, picked out by the evening sunshine. But all of this tranquil nature was in complete contrast to the technological trauma that was unfolding in the caravan.

The battery on the laptop had stopped working, so we could only use the computer if it was plugged into the mains in the caravan. This would have posed no problem had the mobile phone that we were using as an internet hotspot not stopped working as well.

We had been sold the phone on the basis that we could use it to get internet abroad and indeed we could – but only on the phone. We had purchased the phone contract with huge amounts of data for the express purpose of using it as an internet hotspot on a 3-month European trip. However, the salesperson who selected the perfect contract to meet our needs had omitted to mention that "tethering" the phone to the computer to use it as a hotspot is not permitted abroad!

It was in the small print of the contract, which the very helpfully unhelpful helpdesk in India kept telling us. We kept telling THEM that this wasn't the point! We had carefully explained our requirements to the salesperson – and YOU try answering long emails and writing blogs on a phone. Even the weather forecast wouldn't display properly on the screen, but faced with the usual intransigence of Big Business towards its customers, we had no choice but to live with it.

The irony was that I think that it was the act of looking on a French website for a laptop battery that had alerted our phone provider to the fact that we were in France. We had only done that because Mr Bricolage advised via the medium of mime that laptop batteries were way beyond the remit of a local, village hardware store. Worse, I had foolishly done a free computer upgrade to Windows 10. I should have known that there was no such thing as a free upgrade. Now NOTHING on the computer worked properly unless it was online!

With no battery, taking the laptop to the Wi-Fi hotspot at the campsite reception was not an option. However, buying an English / French socket adapter from Mr Bricolage did mean that we could take the laptop to L' Auberge du Petit Matelot, plug into the mains and use their Wi-Fi for the cost of a coffee. Phew! We needed to file my Tax Return and we appeared to have an outstanding water bill. We felt like Master Criminals on the run with Bournemouth Water on our tails, threatening legal action for an unpaid bill that we had never actually received!

One of the more technically-minded windsurfers, Mike, came over to help us to get our newly-purchased-for-the-trip satellite dish working. We had tried ourselves, but the instructions were written in "English As She Is Spoke" and made no sense whatsoever. Mike did suss that we had connected the satellite dish to the caravan, but not to the television! We still didn't get it working but managed to download a Satellite Finder app onto the phone. This caused the phone, our only working piece of tech, to lock. Merde!

We had experienced much caravan-envy when people came in to have a look at our new mobile home. Most admired the beautiful picture windows at the front; the large fridge; the four-ring hob, oven and microwave or the dinky little bathroom at the back. My favourite so far, however, was Mike walking in and asking immediately "Can I look at your fuse box?" I do wonder if anyone, ever has complimented the fuse box on a Bailey Unicorn Vigo quite as comprehensively as Mike!

The next drama was with poor Ruby, who sliced open her pad when we were walking on the beach. This necessitated a trip to the vet - and the deployment of my French Language Skills from school, which had been dormant for forty years! Despite coping miraculously well with this, I decided to officially resign from all shopping and cooking duties. Buoyed by the success of the fresh market mackerel with new potatoes, served with wild fennel that had I foraged on our walk, I subsequently cooked up the most expensive fish in the world (€38 for 2 fish. I nearly fainted.) I followed up with an uncooked oven-baked Filet de Julienne with Onion and Coriander, a rump steak that I discovered was actually horse - and then Galette de Bretagne with garlic mushrooms and a Greek salad. It would have been perfect; if only the pancakes that I had bought had not been sweet.

It wasn't just our vegetarian friends who were disgusted that we ate horse. We didn't tell anyone that we enjoyed it, although we didn't give any to the dogs. It would have felt wrong to have two of our favourite creatures eating each other!

My other shopping success was a piece of hose that I bought for rinsing salt and sand off the dogs following their play sessions on the beach. It didn't seem to work at all. When we connected it up, we discovered that it was blocked. There was what appeared to be a bung in the end! Then, we thought that the sudden water pressure against the blockage had burst the hose since water also seemed to be leaking out all over. We cut it to try to salvage a length without any holes in. "Who puts a bung in a hosepipe?" we were asking in our best "I don't BELIEVE it!" voices. Then it dawned on us that what I had purchased was actually a garden irrigation system.

As the weeks passed, we started to get used to our new lifestyle and came to terms with having lots of plans for the day - and then not doing any of them! Sometimes, we would have a lazy morning, an afternoon nap and then a relaxing evening. It felt strange that, although we had been off the work treadmill for a year and a half, we still retained a nagging work ethic that made us believe that we should be achieving something all the time. We agreed that we should be doing EXACTLY what we wanted to do. We had to keep reminding ourselves – THAT was what we had worked for all those years to achieve!

We ordered a little rubber bootie for Ruby from the vet, as she had to keep her injured paw dry. She became a lot less depressed once she could go outside a bit more with her boot on. We knew that walking on her sore paw might delay her recovery, but I couldn't bear her not being our little ray of sunshine. She had started singing to us again in the morning and her tail had been wagging a bit. She even jumped up, squealed and gnawed my nose. That was definitely much more like our little Princess!

We returned to the market in St Jean. We felt like we're visiting the butcher in The League of Gentlemen, Hilary Briss, for some of his "special stuff" (the unspoken assumption in the comedy show is that "special stuff" is of human origin!) We went to the horse butcher and bought another horse rump steak AND some horse "bavette" (skirt). Now tasked with all cooking and shopping, Mark's trip to Super U yielded two mackerel for €6, so he was slowly making up my €38 fish deficit!

With Mark on cooking detail, I agreed to wash up. That was a bad idea. We were still copying everyone else and not using the facilities in the caravan. I took a bowl of pots to the washing up area, pre-rinsed everything, washed it all, rinsed the soap off – then dropped the whole bally lot on the concrete. Mark said that he heard the crash. I was just furious that I had dropped it AFTER I had washed it all. If I only had just broken everything straight away, I could have saved myself all that work!

Commenting later on the incident, Mark said; "I instantly knew it was you. As I heard the crash, the first thought that crossed my mind was, 'Oh, I had better go and help Jackie to clear up.'" I said that he was one to talk; I had only broken two plates, a Pyrex dish and a cup. I know the plates were Wedgewood, but we were only using our best china in the caravan because he broke our whole "everyday" dinner service when it fell out of the back door of the van! "It's going to take me a long time to live that down." He said. Yes Mark. It is!

Victoria Wood once said that she didn't understand caravanning as a vacation concept. She referred to caravanners as "A bunch of people who can't go on holiday without their own dish brush." Well. I'd like you to know that we certainly don't fall into THAT category. We have TWO dish brushes!

By now, we had been in Penthièvre for three weeks. We had been forced to hang around for a while to wait for the delivery of our laptop battery from Amazon. The battery duly arrived and we kept saying that we were going to leave, but with the sun, sand and good company (of both the human and canine kind) we keep putting it off. We had been supposed to leave AGAIN on Tuesday - until we saw the wind forecast for the week and decided that it would be rude.

Our road trip seemed to have become defined by not actually going anywhere!

9

A POSTCARD FROM PENTHIÈVRE - PART 2

Lost At Sea; French by Numbers; More Culinary Capers...

Greg, our Best Man asked us if we were sure that we would survive this trip and I must admit, I did wonder. Our caravan learning curve had certainly involved a lot of destruction, although Mark calling me clumsy was like the pot and the kettle. He came in from a windsurfing session looking a bit sheepish. "I just had to self-rescue..." he admitted. He had forgotten to screw his sail on to his board, so when he gained a bit of speed, the whole rig had come away in his hand!

Rosie had been busy developing new skills. Mostly along the lines of escape artistry. We didn't always know how she was getting out, but we had personally observed a disappearing act which included jumping out of the windows, over the half-door and burrowing under the awning. I think that the only caravan orifices through which she hadn't escaped were the roof lights!

Our Dutch neighbours commented on how well-behaved our fur family was and asked us if the dogs had been to training classes. "Who do you hear us calling back the most often?" we asked them. "Row-see." they replied. "She is the only one who went to training…" we admitted – and her independent-mindedness was exactly why! Rosie had networked her own little social circle of dogs to visit around the campsite, so we were getting better at finding her when she did escape. She was particularly fond of the two ladies on the hill with their sweet little Papillon, Aloha.

Our neighbour, Françoise, had also taken to our pups. She started doggie-sitting them for us so that Mark and I could windsurf together. She told us that they were "Adorable!" and very well behaved, but I think that the bout of obedience had a lot to do with the 'saucisson' with which she plied them. She had their characters taped. She said that Kai was "le plus calme" and Lani was "la plus terrible!" Our little minxy-munchkin the most terrible? Surely not!

During my windsurfing sessions, I seemed to end up racing the same French bloke most of the time. Then, one evening, my nemesis came over to the caravan to inspect my kit. He was quite a large, middle-aged man and he brought with him the most minute Yorkshire terrier. It put me in mind of receiving a visit from Obelix and Dogmatix from the Asterix cartoons.

While it had covered visiting the vet, the fishmonger and a hardware store with mixed success, my French vocabulary didn't really encompass the technicalities of windsurfing. Nevertheless, we managed a perfectly gentile conversation – by numbers! We discussed our relative sail sizes; "Vous, sept-cinque. Moi, huite-six." he told me; "You 7.5, me 8.6m." Then board sizes; "Cent dix – 110L" We decided in sign language that anything smaller might sink.

We mulled on the surprising width of my board "soix-ant-quinze – 75cm." Mon Dieu! We concurred that it was also quite short for the width. We agreed in mime that we had both been on the right sized kit for the conditions and that it had been a bit choppy, which was rough on the knees. Then, with a few more Gallic head nods and shrugs, he and his tiny dog departed.

I discovered later that this was Gilles – a seasonal regular and great friend of many of the English windsurfers in Penthièvre. I took him by surprise when I introduced myself later. I learned that his tiny dog was called Attila – his family name was something like Dahun, hence Attila Dahun!

3rd August – Ha ha, we were "definitely leaving tomorrow, come what may." Apart from full sun and 20 knots of wind... I un-cooked dinner again, cursing the slowness of the caravan oven when it took an hour-and-a-half to cook a pork fillet rather than thirty minutes, even when I turned it up to full. I realised later that it was cooking so slowly, even on full, because the gas bottle had run out.

4th August – We Hit The Road Jack... "Don't get lost at sea!" joked Françoise as she waved us off on our windsurfers, while deftly dishing out slices of saucisson to the hounds. "As if!" I quipped. I think, however, that Mark had planned revenge for my cooking. It was a perfect last windsurf session and I was so powered up that I left Mark for dead on one reach (he claimed later that he hadn't noticed!) As the Captain of my ship, it was, of course, my responsibility to ensure that my vessel was seaworthy. Still, as Mark had said when his own sail came off in his hands, it is always good to keep up your self-rescue skills. Mark had rigged my sail and as such, I should really thank him for not tightening up my UJ (Universal Joint – it connects the sail to the board), which meant that my sail and board parted company half a mile offshore.

Thankfully, I was under the watchful eye of Gilles and with some help from Mark, who eventually noticed that I was floundering in the water rather than overtaking him, managed to re-connect everything and sail safely back to land.

It was quite emotional leaving Penthièvre. We had been there for six weeks in the end and with so many seasonal residents, it was beginning to feel like home. Gilles came along to wave us off along with our Dutch neighbours, who wouldn't let us leave without having a last cup of coffee with them. They laughed and reminded us "You were leaving three weeks ago!" Françoise had a tear in her eye and the little dog Aloha came to kiss us goodbye with her two mums "Jusqu'à l'année prochaine! – 'til next year!" they all shouted as we drove away.

After losing my rig sailing last night, Gilles quipped in a grinning Gallic mime "Make sure that Mark has connected the caravan to the van..."

It was just as well that I did check because Mark had, in fact, forgotten to connect the ALKO – and no, that is not my intravenous drip of local wine – it is the anti-snake stabilising device.

And so it was that finally, with the caravan and van properly hitched, our road trip actually hit the road!

10

AVANTON, POITIERS – PAYS DU FUTUROSCOPE

We Meet Celebrities; Really EARN that Yorkie Bar & Endure an Aquaroll Approximation.

Well, I had finally earned my Yorkie bar! I had driven The Big Rig in France for the first time, including a successful reverse and controlling a few incipient snakes which were triggered when overtaking lorries.

As we left Penthièvre, the plan had been to go down the coast of Brittany to the Atlantic islands; Îles de Ré, Noirmoutier and Oléron. We decided on a whim to turn east instead of south and go inland. Our six happy weeks in Penthièvre meant that it was now the mad, mad month of August, when the whole of Europe goes on holiday. We figured that inland would be a bit less crowded than the coast.

Now that we had finally got around to it, we were glad that we had moved on. It was refreshing to see a different landscape and wonderful to be in green countryside and forest. I don't know about the sands of time, but we were relieved to be away from the sands of Penthièvre – particularly those delivered copiously by the Sandman (in canine form) into our bed each night!

We were in Aquitaine, where Richard the 1st's Mum, Eleanor hailed from. It is an area where places are named after celebrities; there is Poitiers, obviously named after the famous actor, Sidney. Then there is Loudun, brother of Rufus - one of the musical Wainwright brothers from America; (not related to Alfred Wainwright, Blackburn's famous son; immortalised by his illustrated mountain guide books, a bridge over the Leeds-Liverpool canal and a fine pint of bitter from local brewers Thwaite's.)

The countryside here reminded me of Dorset, only with fields full of sunflowers and an abundance of rambling, stone Chateaux. We were in wine country, staying in AOC Haut-Poitou, near the Saumur Nord Vienne, Loire and Maine. Salut!

On our first evening, I took the doggies for a walk up into the fields and watched the sunset. The fields smelled of straw; the scent was carried on the lightest summer breeze, which made the wild flowers bob their heads. It was beautiful. I saw a deer bound across a field and watched a hot air balloon hang like a shadowy bauble in the orange sky. It was such a lovely area, with oodles of walking and an abundance of cycle ways.

The Pays du Futuroscope, as the area is known (in honour of its Theme Park!) seemed to be one of those places a bit like The Borders in Scotland – people pass through on their way to somewhere else and miss out. We decided to stay longer than our proposed one night and giggled when we realised that against our original outline "plan", we should already have crossed France, spent two weeks in the mountains in Samoëns and be on our way back!

On Sunday, we had planned to get up early and go to

Poitiers, so instead, we went to the market at Neuville-de-Poitou.

The weather was scorching, with temperatures in the high 30°s, so in the afternoon, we relaxed in the shade and filled the paddling pool for the dogs to cool off. We debated what we thought had been their favourite experience of the day; the live pig at the charcuterie stall, sticking their heads into a lady's shopping basket - or BATH TIME.

It had been too hot to walk until 9pm, by which time we had emptied a bottle of Haut Poitou wine purchased at reception while sitting outside and chatting away in the balmy evening air. It was going on for midnight before it was cool enough to even think about sleep.

It was at the campsite in Avanton that I discovered at least one of the reasons that everyone immediately replies to me in English when I try to speak French. I was filling up our Aquaroll water carrier. "Bonjour" I said, just as the bloke approaching said "Hello" simultaneously. "I never know which to say!" I quipped, "Only ze English use zose." he said, indicating my Aquaroll.

I relayed this conversation to Mark later "It's not my terrible accent." I gushed. "They reply in English because of the Aquaroll!" "What's an Aquaroll?" asked my Competent Caravanner husband.

It turns out that Mark thought that an Aquaroll was a way of rolling your Rs, like you do when you speak Italian. Rrrrrrrr!

Monday was a bit cooler and cloudier, so it seemed like a good idea to go into Poitiers. However, we lost the will to live when we got caught in the gravitational pull of the Périphérique and a one-way system that kept spitting us out in the same place on each of our many attempts to enter the city limits. We could clearly SEE an open car park, but we could only get to a car park with a 2m height barrier, which was absolutely no good for our van with all our surf boards stacked on the roof rack.

By then, we'd seen as much of Poitiers as we wanted to, so we went to Loudun instead. It was really pretty but reminded me of the time Mark and I visited Glasgow – and could not find a pub!

Here we were in a touristy city in France and there was not one, single, pretty pavement café in sight. We walked around the deserted streets. It was August, so everyone was away on holiday – but clearly not in Loudon. We had an interesting conversation in French outside the church with Christine. We discussed Brexit; the many shortcomings of the EU; ageing (with particular emphasis on keeping your marbles); the widening gap between rich and poor; dogs, of course and how hard it is when you lose a pet... She loved our pups, particularly Rosie. She showed us where she lived and told us to come and visit her again!

We ended up having lunch at a truck stop on the main road back to Poitiers. €14 for deux sandwich (jambon in a dry baguette) and deux boisson (in cans). It was expensive and hardly the al fresco treat that I had envisaged, but by then it was 3pm and I was so hungry that it was worth every cent.

We moved on to Guesnes and enjoyed a beautiful walk in the Forêt de Scevolles. In an area which houses the second most popular theme park in France, The Futuro-scope, it was wonderful, in high season, to go to a tourist attraction and see not one other living soul! The forest was fragrant and tranquil, with beautiful Acacia trees and wooden sculptures dotted around. From The Pawsome

Foursome's point of view, it was heaven. We had bathed them on Sunday and they smelled deliciously of Almond shampoo. Like sightseeing, however, almond fragrance was not acceptable to them. "Why are you dragging us round a boring town when we can go to a lovely forest? (And roll in poo!)" I have to say I am largely in agreement with them – although they did just sneak in that bit about rolling in poo.

On Tuesday, we had a grand plan to go and walk in a beautiful area near a river but we found a tick on Lani. For some reason after we removed it, she went lame! Our poor little love was limping really badly. We decided to do the laundry instead but realised that with all the faffing with the tick, 12:00 had come and gone. The significance of this was that reception had closed. We dealt with the two hour closure admirably, by going back to bed and enjoying a siesta until reception re-opened to allow us to purchase a token which allowed us to use the washing machine.

Laundry was interrupted by each individual dog in succession coming to find me in the laverie and then everyone joining in a game of ball with a lady and her two daughters, who had originally come to do their washing up! Chatting with them about the breed, it turns out that the French for 'Poodle' is not 'Poodle', but 'Caniche'. I keep mixing up the word 'Caniche' with 'Cornichon' - and am in severe danger of explaining to the many people who ask that the pups are a cross between a Cavalier King Charles Spaniel and a Gherkin.

We finally went out at 4pm to drive to a walk by the river, but we found that there wasn't really much river to be had. We sat for a while on the only piece of bank to which we had access and watched a kingfisher, which was a bonus. Then we drove back off-piste and decided that we would move on the following day, so we packed up and made ready.

Little did we know that we were about to discover The True Secret of a Successful Relationship!

11

ARGENTON SUR CREUSE – A HOLD UP WITH A HAIRPIN!

How to Maintain a Successful Relationship When You Drive Each Other Round the Bend.

10th August – we drove for about three-and-a-half hours from Avanton to Argenton on minor roads. It was really enjoyable passing through picture-perfect villages - and it obviously made my day to drive through St Julien l'Ars!

I was at the wheel all the way, coping admirably with overhanging rocks and a narrow railway bridge. I only met my match when the caravan Sat Nav faced us with a proper hairpin.

The Sat Nav is supposed to take into account our height and length when planning routes. Until now, it had been worth its weight in gold. While Mark might claim that I drive him around the bend, I failed to do so on this particular occasion. I am pleased to say, however, that even when I got in the right side of the van for a girl (the passenger seat) Mark didn't manage to drive me around the bend either!

I think we entertained the lady in the house opposite, however. I got the impression that she lay in wait for unsuspecting long vehicles on their way to the campsite, because her face just seemed to be there; disembodied and hovering at the window with her grey hair scraped back in a bun.

As we got to the bend, she showed no emotion as she watched each of us in turn;

1. Try to get around the bend by taking it wide (not enough room);
2. Try to get around the bend by doing a 3-point turn with a mid-point mini-reverse (not enough room);
3. Try to reverse up a hill on a narrow track opposite (the caravan almost grounded - and there was not enough room!)

Once we had exhausted all of the entertaining options, the face at the window beckoned me over and told me that if we just went straight on, there was a car park up the road that we could use to turn round. "C'est plus facile!" – "It's much easier!" she said. She didn't even crack a smile.

"Why, thank you for your timely sharing of advice, Madam." I felt like saying.

Her face, impassive, was still floating in her window on our second pass, so we gave her a friendly wave. The irony was that the campsite was NOT up the hairpin ANYWAY, but back somewhere along the road on which we had come. However, we both agreed that the Sat Nav had omitted to call that particular left turn.

And therein we discovered the secret to a successful relationship. Sometimes you DO need to drive each other round the bend – you just need to check that it's the right bend first!

As we pulled into Campsite les Chambons, it looked

idyllic. It was right next to the River Creuse and fifteen minutes' walk along the river to Argenton "The Venice of the Berry". After telling reception that we would "stay perhaps 'til Monday" we walked into Argenton and can only say that we were underwhelmed!

Starting life as the Roman "Argentomagus", there are medieval streets to explore in Argenton, but the gorgeous river walk from our campsite lasted for only about 100 yards before entering the industrial rear end of the town. We ignored the litter along the riverbank, which looked as though it might contain the remains of drug paraphernalia and concentrated on the evening reflections on the surface of the river, which were very beautiful.

We were glad of our on-board facilities in the caravan, since the camp toilets were not working; there was only one disabled cubicle available to serve the entire site. However, we slept soundly to the soothing lullaby of water rushing over a small weir on the river, right next to the caravan.

So after remaining stationary on our travels for six weeks, we were suddenly starting to hare across France, but we definitely needed to improve our score on river walks!

Moving on meant that we had to forgo the pleasure of a visit to the Musée Chemiserie – the Shirt Museum in Argenton.

Having once planned a whole holiday to Italy around an Umbrella Museum near Stresa that we had read about in our "Italian for Idiots" book, it was disappointing not to be able to add this little gem to our demented depository of Mad Museums.

Nevertheless, it is occasions such as this that are the reason to have a mobile home. If you don't like your location or your neighbours, you move on.

And what a move it was!

12

DIGOIN, LOIRE – NOW THAT'S WHAT I CALL A RIVER WALK!

Caravan Envy; A National Identity Crisis; The Lollipop Ladies &
The Ship in the Sky!

11th **August** – We had been working our way up French
rivers by way of importance and had now hit the Loire. We
arrived via countryside which still looked like Dorset and
Hampshire, apart from the muscular, white Charolais cattle
shimmering in the sun-kissed fields.

We had another little reversing incident as we arrived at
Camping le Chevrette. A few Dutch caravanners pulled up
their pews in anticipation but we gave an excellent account
of ourselves. We had tried to secure a pitch right next to the
Loire in what we realised too late was a caravan NO GO
zone. Caravan Confucius insists – "ALWAYS WALK SITE
AND SCOPE OUT PITCH!"

To get out of our predicament we had to reverse back the
way we had come, which was downhill and around a corner,
avoiding the gable end of the toilet block roof by a whisker.
The Dutch were very admiring of Mark's driving skills and I
detected some Caravan Envy of our beautiful Kismet.

.   .   .

As FAR AS the river walks went, it was third time lucky. The Loire definitely delivered! We walked along its meandering banks and the doggies had a cool off in the shallow, languid waters. We saw another kingfisher as we promenaded into town through a shady avenue of plane trees. We did a double take when we saw a boat high in the sky, crossing the Loire via the town bridge. We went to investigate – and did our first ever traverse of an aqueduct. There was LOADS of walking and cycling in the area. It was such a lovely location that we decided to stay a while!

Later, our fur babies acted as a magnet to every child on the campsite. A multi-national contingent of rug rats turned up at our caravan, each tucking into a Smarties ice-cream. The posse included Elodie, who was bespectacled, quiet and permanently clad in a pink cycle helmet although not always accompanied by a bike. Tish was the ringleader and sported an ever-changing rainbow of lollipop stains around her mouth. The preponderance of colours from the red end of the spectrum led us to understand that berries and fruits-of-the-forest fell among her favourite flavours.

In Tish, you could not have hoped to meet a lovelier child. She was polite and considerate enough to ask if she should take her entourage away while we set up the caravan. We thanked her and told her to come back in an hour. She was back 60-minutes later, to the second, accompanied by a few more of her friends. She wanted to know all about the dogs; "Are Rosie and Kai lovers?" and "Can they make babies?" I said no and she asked "Il est castré?" – very worldly-wise. I don't think that one needs any translation!

Tish had told us that one of the little girls in her posse

was Dutch and didn't understand French. We had been communicating with her in sign language for a few days before we discovered that she was, in fact, English! We met her family and they explained that as the whole sign language charade had continued, she had become too embarrassed to admit that she was English, so had just run with it. Although we learned that Tish had also told her that WE were Dutch... It would seem that our minimal grasp of the native language rather than "shouting loudly at foreigners" marked us out straight away as "can't possibly be Brits..."

The weather map of France looked like the chart on The Fast Show's Channel 9; "SCORCHIO!" On Monday, the mercury had hit 37°C. We stayed around the campsite and took our SUPs (Stand Up Paddle Boards) on the river. We had all four dogs on the boards. There were some small rapids downstream. Of course, Mark had to go and shoot them! I didn't see what happened, but witnessed him carrying the board back upstream, from which I surmised it hadn't gone altogether successfully. We both took a leisurely paddle upstream to the aqueduct with the Pups on SUPs.

A Californian lady pitched a tiny, retro caravan next door to us. She was towing with a beaten-up old Volvo. We exchanged only the niceties of a first meeting, but in this briefest of conversations, she still managed to muscle in the fact that "My other caravan is an Airstream but it's too expensive to tow with my Mercedes around Europe for months on end." I wondered if it was because America is just more materialistic or whether our Bailey had once again provoked Caravan Envy.

Although we could have legitimately claimed "We dine from NOTHING but Wedgewood in the caravan!" we omitted to mention that what she was looking at was actually pretty much everything that we owned in the whole world.

13

CHALLES LES EAUX – AVOIDING THE PAINS OF AIX!

Vulcanicity, the Debut Ding - plus Perceptions of Proper Peaks!

"12-Across. What is the highest point in England (8,4)?"

Our last morning in Digoin, we were chatting to an American chap over a coffee as he wrestled with his crossword.

"Scafell Pike (**SEVEN, 4**)" we replied. So it appears that both we and the Ordnance Survey have got the spelling wrong. According to the erudite annals of the New York Times, we had both missed out the 'R' in 'Scarfell.' What IDIOTS!

"We've had some spectacular thunderstorms since we started caravanning!" we replied in answer to his question as to whether Britain experiences thunderstorms. "But in the UK, everything is a little small-scale and Mickey Mouse compared to America."

We explained that British thunderstorms were nothing like those that he would see in his home state of Virginia. "A hot day like today (33°C) would probably make the British newspapers, with the headline "Phew! What a Scorcher!"

And Scafell Pike is not even 4000-feet high, never mind metres." He looked impressively unimpressed.

But talking about mountains, we had reached them now. The proper mountains. The big pointy ones with snow on the top - which should be the law!

We had crossed Central France, which, as I reported, looked like Hampshire but with sunflowers and Chateaux. We entered the Maconnaise, which reminded me of the conifer-clad foothills of Wales near Llangollen. We encountered limestone country – the Bugey valley, a bit like Malham but with MILES of blue-grey and pink walls, soaring ever higher. The trees were just beginning to change; autumn here would probably rival New England. Caravan Confucius say; "Those who travel find many place to come back to!"

We had squinted as we came out of Le Tunnel du Chat into bright sunshine and there they were. The lofty peaks of the Savoie. A landscape that looks like nothing else. We felt quite at home. We have skied there so often that we even own a "bag for life" from the Super U in Haut Savoie!

Once again, our rivers had been rising; in importance, at least. Today we had opened the bidding with the Loire, raised it via the Saône and had now reached the mighty Rhône. We were also in another wine region. Damn that planning. And isn't there a saying "When in Rhône...?" Cheers!

We only dinged the caravan slightly coming off a tricky pitch and dinged it not at all getting into a "you're having a laugh!" pitch. Luckily Mark kept a cool head reversing around picnic tables, trees and park benches with the eyes of everyone on site boring into him.

We had grounded out the back of the caravan as we left the last campsite at Digoin – it was the tiniest incline but with a long caravan and the laws of leverage, it is surprising how slight the incline needs to be to cause the back to hit the deck. The damage popped the nearside rear trim off its screws and was easily fixed, but it was our first ding. I was particularly distressed because it had happened on my watch. As you would expect, heading for the hills, it was a difficult journey, with a lot of winding roads. I do believe that when we arrived, we had earned that wine.

We had planned to stop at Aix les Bains, a spa town on Lake Bourget, France's largest freshwater lake. However, when we got there, it was hideous. It reminded us of Blackpool, only with sunshine.

It was tasteless in the extreme; busy, noisy and full of brightly coloured umbrellas and pedalos. Not only that, had we wanted to stay there, the campsite charged 33% more than anywhere else for the displeasure, so we carried on! We reached Challes les Eaux, another spa town. There was no lake – no pedalos, but Campsite Municipal Le Savoy nestled quietly and spectacularly under the mountains. That was much more like it!

18th **August – RAIN!** It was only our second day of rain since we had come to Europe and with the mercury having hovered consistently at around 37°C – it was glorious.

Mark made me smile. We were enjoying a coffee in our treasured Vulcan XH558 mugs as we played Led Zeppelin's "The Rain Song"; a crisp, guitar-led accompaniment to the sound of raindrops pounding on the caravan roof.

The Vulcan is one of my favourite aeroplanes. Her technology and delta wing design was the precursor to Concorde. "It's odd that they named the Vulcan after a race of fictional beings." Mark ventured. I nearly choked! "That's illogical, Captain. It's named after Vulcan, the Roman god of fire, who pre-dates Star Trek by several thousand years!"

Built in 1956, the plane itself also pre-dates Star Trek by almost exactly a decade. However, I love the idea that my favourite plane was named after Mr Spock, who is, in fact, also my favourite Vulcan! (Well, half-Vulcan if we're being pedantic, which Trekkies are. Always.)

We had lunch of Cake Jambon Fromage and it was just that. A cheesy sponge cake with bits of ham and green olives in it. It was, er, different! It faired up in the afternoon, so we drove up to Curiene and walked up to the little chapel on Mont St Michel.

I just love being in the mountains, they always make me feel so alive. The views were stunning and we experienced that amazing sense of altitude that you get when you see aircraft actually flying beneath you. There was a whole posse of gliders rising silently on thermals, but they had some way to ascend to reach our lofty eyrie.

But the best thing about Challes? We rather wished that we had saved some laundry for this campsite – un jeton laver linge (a washing machine token) was only €3 here. What a bargain! The cheapest we had found so far was €4 and to date, it had been mostly €5 per load.

When travelling on a budget, one has such things to consider!

14

THE END OF THE LINE – SIXT FER-À-CHEVAL

Flash floods, Unlucky Jim, Killer Sheepdogs – & The Kamikaze Chemi Khazi!

19th **August** – We found ourselves beneath a bowl of mighty peaks, so close to Switzerland that we could have yodelled over Les Dents Blanches to order a cuckoo clock. The views were amazing; rocky peaks that touched the clouds, patched by bright green hanging valleys with snow-melt cascades free-falling for thousands of feet down their sheer, limestone walls.

We had finally crossed the whole of France and had reached the end of the line; the head of the Giffre valley. The only way forward from here was straight over the top of 3000m peaks and into the land of the holey cheese.

We were a little bit wary of the campsite's rather "League of Gentlemen" warning about evacuation. In the "unlikely" event of flash flooding, it said that we would need "to leave in walking, bring only passports, money and precious things – and leave the car and equipment of campsite."

I had caused some consternation getting Caravan

Kismet off our tricky pitch in Challes. There was a hairy moment for the gathered crowd when they saw me climb into the driver's seat. Then I backed successfully onto the hitch. I had considered performing elaborate manoeuvres with Big Blue to avoid the leaning trees, bench and table tennis table; in the end, I disappointed my public by simply pulling Kismet onto the road and pivoting her by hand. Then, I got my fixed flange ball in position perfectly, first time. So there was "nothing to see here."

Bloody women drivers!

It was quite funny rocking up at Campsite Municipal le Pelly in a huge caravan. We were miles from anywhere and all the people on the campsite were hardy mountain types in tiny tents or slightly battered micro-caravans. We are British though. We have a stereotype of latent eccentricity to uphold. Maybe the fact that we had unknowingly marinated all our vegetables in cooking brandy (the bottle emptied itself in transit) could aid our cause in this direction. Our potatoes now smelled like a pub the morning after!

And OK - I admit it. WE USED SOME TOLL ROADS ON THIS LEG. Big Blue was a bit hot-under-the-bonnet when we arrived in Challes les Eaux. Her oil and water were fine, so we figured that it could be her clutch, which had obviously seen a lot of action on the twisting mountain roads. We thought that a few tolls would be considerably more economical than a burnt out clutch. However, €16 – a night's campsite fee - to cover 60 miles shows how quickly toll charges can rack up.

We passed some graffiti demanding that the Savoie be released from French oppression. It is certainly an area with a distinct personality, which is not surprising when you consider its history. The River Giffre, which gives its name to the valley where we were staying, takes its name from the

Burgonde word meaning "Big Water". The Burgondes were a Germanic people of Scandinavian origin who, in 443, created a kingdom in what is now Savoie, with Geneva as their capital.

Sixt, the village where we pitched up, is probably better known as a ski resort. It is part of the Grand Massif ski area, which is the fourth largest in France. Our campsite was at 1000m and by accident, we managed to avoid the rookie mistake of caravanning at altitude – the exploding toilet! Luckily, I opened a bottle of fizzy water and it reminded me about pressure differences and the importance of pressure equalisation between the exterior and the interior of the sealed toilet cassette. In a wine area of the calibre of Savoie, a caravan toilet was WAY down my list of methods of, well, to put it bluntly, getting sh** faced!

After managing to level Kismet on the mountainside by shoring up our levelling ramps with foraged bits of wood, we went for a lovely, evening walk around the Cirque du Fer-à-Cheval. We ascended above the river. The roar of rushing water got louder as we got further away from the river as it was amplified by the natural amphitheatre of the rock walls. Then, as we strolled on through the woods and alpine meadows, the chirping crickets were so loud that they drowned out even the augmented sound of the river!

We felt beautifully relaxed, drinking in the majesty of the jaw-droppingly high mountains. Then we saw a sign telling us to beware of the guard dogs released to protect the sheep flocks from lynx and wolves. The sign warned us to approach these dogs with caution; we truly were out in the wilds. I was not sure which was the scariest prospect; lynx, wolves – or the dogs running free who are capable of seeing off such top-level predators!

The Sixt Fer-à-Cheval (Sixt Horseshoe) is the largest

limestone amphitheatre in Europe. It is 5km long and rises to 2985m on the summit of Tenneverge. Mysterious underground rivers emerge from the mountainside and cascade spectacularly down the rock walls. They are probably meltwaters from the glaciers, although in truth, no-one is sure of their exact source.

One of the waterfalls is called the Fontaine de l'Or – "The Fountain of Gold". Another is less romantically called the "Cascade de Pissevache". If that means what I think it does, I suppose that in its own Bovine way, it also refers to a golden fountain!

You have heard of "La Vache qui Rie; The Laughing Cow" – those ubiquitous, plastic cheese triangles. A bit of clever product placement, possibly beverage related – what about "La Vache qui Pee"? Along with my idea for a chain of restaurants with miserable waiters called "The Unhappy Eater" I will give you that one. I think it would sell!

We saw an information sign stating that the first person to ascend Mont Blanc, Jacques Balmat, spent most of his life looking for gold in the mountains surrounding Sixt Fer-à-Cheval and Vallorcine. He died there in 1834, aged 72. While iron was later found and extracted in small quantities from the mountains, gold has never been found (other than in the naming of the waterfalls!)

We later read the less-romantic-not-for-the-tourists version of poor Jacques' life. His daughter had died as he was making his first ascent of Mont Blanc and all his money, including his prize for the first ascent, was stolen.

Jacques and his partner Pache had been looking for gold in Sixt following a rumour that a man from the Valais had found gold in the hoof of an ibex that he had shot. They set off towards the glacier but Pache returned alone. Jacques never was never seen again. The speculation was that he fell down a crevasse. Jacques' body was never recovered and there was a theory that having discovered a seam of gold, his partner had pushed him into the void.

His great-nephew, who launched an expedition to find out what happened to Jacques, also died in the Sixt valley following an illness.

Iron is very much in evidence in the area and the likelihood is that if anything was discovered, it was Iron Pyrites – Iron Disulphide or "Fools' Gold". Jacques is the French equivalent of the name James, so he really was Unlucky Jim.

Iron has actually been mined in Sixt since 1655, although generally not with any great commercial success. The English took over eventually and with astute British inventiveness, they devised a brilliant system to save time and manpower. Instead of men carrying heavy baskets of iron ore down the mountain on their backs, they opted to hurl it down from the summit of the Boret. The local farmers, fearing damage to their alpine pastures reacted strongly... Iron mining in Sixt was soon abandoned.

But this is PROOF of early European interference with Elf and Safety!

And unequivocal evidence that our predecessors upheld the idea of English eccentricity in Sixt CENTURIES before we came on the scene with our feeble offering of a caravan filled with brandy-soaked potatoes.

15

MONDAY – MARVEL, MORILLON, MUTTS & MOUNTAINS!

Sixt Fer-à-Cheval is located in a beautiful area, which boasts walks, wildlife and waterfalls. However, 85% of Sixt falls within the Natural Reserve of Sixt-Passy; the largest Natural Reserve in the Haute Savoie. Like many French National Parks and Reserves, dogs are not allowed off- or even on-lead in many areas, so it is not a place where you can expect to be able to trek hut-to-hut over a glacier with your canine companions.

The closest walk to our campsite, the Cirque du Sixt-Fer-à-Cheval, was definitely leads-on (and dogs were permitted only part of the way – as far as the refuge at Buvette de Prazon.) We had done our homework, however and had found plenty of walks further down the valley towards Samoëns where, unencumbered by tethers, The Fab Four could run their paws off!

It was Monday. We parked at Morillon 1100 (a ski resort - also known as Les Esserts.) We walked up one of my favourite pistes, the green run "Marvel", which winds around the side of the mountain, affording spectacular views. It was a beautiful, sunny day, so it was delightful that much of the walk was in the shade. We met only people descending. This was because you can ascend the lazy way on the gondola from Samoëns or the chairlift from Morillon. We felt slightly superior making the climb ourselves, although a chairlift was never really an option with four pooches!

We had a gorgeous and well-deserved treat in The Igloo refuge at the top of the lift. We sneaked in a cheeky beer and I had the most delicious omelette that I have ever tasted (Savoie – with ham and cheese) and Mark had a Croque Madame. It was so good perhaps because it was our first meal out in months. Our appetites had been sharpened by the climb and the clean mountain air - and our meal was accompanied by that ever-so-alpine background melody of cowbells!

We were complimented on the excellent behaviour of our dogs; "Ils sont tres gentile! Tres calme!" – I knew that we were the subject of conversation for quite some time afterwards as I kept hearing "Quatre chiens!" – yes, four dogs. And you wouldn't even have known that they were there!

We continued up to the top of Sairon at 1171m – by far the highest that our mountaineering mongrels have ever been. We descended past the bottom of a most treacherous black ski run, La Lanche, which continued further down the slope as a summer mountain bike run – also graded black.

As when we had first skied La Lanche, we thought that it didn't look so bad from the top, but believe me, once you had dropped in and committed, it got very, very much worse! There was no way that I could have cycled it. Steep, narrow and very rough underfoot, it was actually pretty tough to walk.

It was very beautiful, though, strolling down through the peaceful forests with only the sound of rushing water. We were not sure of our bearings; navigation was difficult, but we had seen enough Bear Grylls and Ray Mears survival guides on TV to know that if you "Keep following a water-course, it will bring you to civilisation. Eventually!" I had a heroic injury – my feet, which had been clad in sandals since we left the UK (apart from driving) sustained a blister from wearing proper shoes.

The pups still had enough energy to play on the descent. I have to say that I was getting quite tired. We had been walking for six hours with just a 45-minute stop for lunch, but I am never so happy as I am in the mountains. In perfect weather and with views to die for, this ranked as one of the best mountain days that I have ever had. I get the same buzz from exciting sports such as windsurfing as I do from just being surrounded by the majestic beauty of the mountains. It was also wonderful to see a landscape blossoming in summer that has been so familiar to us under the snows of winter.

It took nearly as long to de-seed our tired doggies when we got back as it did to do the walk! They had spent so much time gambolling in the mountain meadows that they had amassed enough seed in their coats to re-sow a small farm. You know the rhyme – "One man and his dog went to sow a meadow..."

Fresh coffee, old wetsuits and newly mown grass; these are among my favourite aromas. The scent of the grass from these mountain meadows was sweeter here than anywhere else that I have ever been. It is little wonder that local cheeses, such as Reblochon, made from the summer milk of cows grazing these pastures, are so highly prized.

16

TUESDAY – TINES!

Gorgeous Gorges, The Marmite Mystification, plus Zen & the Art of Caravan Conservation

After our six hour and 1,474m epic up Marvel in Morillon on Monday, we felt beautifully beaten up – tired, but happy and in need of a good stretch.

Since it was another dazzling day of full sun, we made plans. I said that I was quite happy to continue with my own plan of lying down and admiring the mountains (we could see magnificent peaks through all of the windows AND through the roof lights!) Mark then planned to make a coffee. We had planned on doing some jobs today; laundry and caravan maintenance but we soon got those off our "To Do" list. We can reveal to you a totally failsafe way of tackling an over-long "To Do" list. Just don't do any of it. Or even better, just cross everything off – then you don't even have to feel guilty!

It was very mindful – our trip had been a blessed relief from the constant need to be "doing". We had been concentrating on "being", although this did mean that we didn't get out for our walk until a much belated 2pm!

We had lunch at the Gorges des Tines. It cost €10 for 1 burger and 1 sandwich jambon-fromage. We had both wanted a burger, but the café had run out of burger buns! We agreed that on a small scale, this demonstrated some of what was wrong with the French economy. We had discovered why all the towns that we visited were so quiet. It was the peak holiday season, so everyone had closed up their business and gone away on holiday! Yet, if you were one of the cunning few who had stayed at home to make the most of the holiday bonanza, why would you bother to stock up on easy-to-store burger buns?

"Tines'" means "cavity" or "pot'". Satisfyingly, the French word for this is "Marmite". The mystical clefts in the rock here provided a landscape that was very different from anywhere else. It was spectacular; damp, mossy, gloomy and green. Needles of sunlight lanced down through the trees and would reach some places for literally just a few seconds each day.

But Marmite is ever controversial and here, a geological "yes or no" rages around this particular one. How were the four roughly parallel fissures formed? There is a theory that they are simply the river beds of the Giffre as she changed course. This could account for one or maybe two but probably not the four Tines, so another theory postulates that they could originate from the torrents of meltwater from the glaciers when the ice-age ended. Love it or hate it, even the *theory* of Marmite has a 50:50 split!

We had intended to walk from the Tines to the Cascade de Rouget but in keeping with today's theme of abandoned plans, there was a fallen tree blocking the route just before a ladder ascent. Mark went to check it out for dog-accessibility (the dogs had already ascended two ladders successfully!) As I waited with the pooches, a group of walkers came past sporting walking poles, boots and proper rucksacks. This was a stark contrast to my sandals, T-shirt and shorts, upon which they commented in French. And which j'ai compris - I understood!

I told them in French that they could get to the ladder past the fallen tree. Strangely, they did not believe me but looked suitably contrite in the knowledge that I had understood their comments about my attire. Then the mad Englishwoman in sandals suddenly proved to them that it was, in fact, feasible to get to the ladder – and very quickly too. The Fab Four suddenly decided that they were missing their Dad. I followed them over and ascended like a rat up a drainpipe, sandoodles an' all, because Lani had started to climb the ladder to go after Mark. Unfortunately, she lost faith halfway up, so I had to rescue her. We decided to leave the Cascade de Rouget for another day - and another route!

This ladder episode reminded me of the charade that had happened yesterday at the car park in Les Esserts. We had to carry all of the pups up a long, metal staircase with mesh steps from the car park to the start of the walk. None of the dogs are keen on mesh bridges or steps. On the way back from our walk, I took a detour via The Sherpa supermarket to score a couple of well-earned beers, while Mark navigated the mesh staircase with the pooches on his own. Clearly, he couldn't carry them all at once, so he did it in stages. First, he relocated Kai to the bottom and told him to wait.

It then became like one of those mathematical puzzles; Mark carried Lani down and told her to wait, but as he went up to collect Rosie, Lani climbed back up again. Lani clearly loves Mark more than she hates stairs! This continued in a pure farce like the Grand Old Duke of York, with Mark and dogs marching up, halfway up and down again – but never quite in synch. Eventually, Mark did get everybody down at the same time and returned to the van – at which point Lani took off to go and search for me!

However, like a Dalek, once she reached the bottom of the staircase again, she suddenly decided that the steps defeated her plan to conquer the Universe. She abandoned her mad heroics and simply ran back to Mark and hopped obediently into the van. Clearly, I am not as valuable a prize as Dad and my esteemed company does not warrant scaling stairs!

As we returned to our campsite through the village of Sixt, we were shocked to see military vehicles and Nazis everywhere. "Where are we? What year is it? Who's the President?" we asked ourselves. Had we experienced a time slip in the Tines? It turned out that they were filming something or other, although it all looked a bit 'Allo 'Allo.

I had purchased a bottle of Cotes du Bergerac wine at the great expense of €4.60. It claimed on the label that "it wins many medals." It was so revolting that even our resident lush Rosie turned up her little wet nose at the vintage! Mark tried one glass and decided in disgust to go and wash the roof of the caravan. The sticky stuff that he had first observed all over the caravan roof in Challes les Eaux appeared now to have solidified into a compound more inert and resistant than diamond, although my Magic Eraser seemed to be making some headway on the worst bits. We considered whether the wine could help to soften it, although it was so acidic that I would have worried that it might dissolve its way through our Alu-tec body shell!

Our French and Dutch neighbours watched intently as Mark gained elevation by standing on the back of Big Blue. I could hear the Dutch chortling away. It seems that a man washing a caravan roof passes for entertainment in the mountains. I will say that with the background of 3000ft peaks, it certainly was the most picturesque vehicle wash ever!

I did Mark a favour by drinking the horrible wine. I didn't want to subject him to any further pain, since while washing the caravan, he managed to slice his finger, stub his toe and spill dog food all over the floor. He had stood on the dog food box to reach through the small middle skylight – in which he had also nearly wedged himself.

With it occupying an unexpected location, I also managed to stub my toe twice on the dog food box and our bed was now soaked. Mark had passed a bowl of water up onto the roof. It did *almost* stay where he put it, but as he proved, gravity is a powerful force which, unlike atmospheric pressure, does not diminish at altitude.

Well, *we* had been warned that this campsite was subject to flash floods. However, we had not expected them to be of our own making!

17

WEDNESDAY – WOOFS & WATERFALLS!

*Freddie Mercury on Wet Weather Camping; Yoda on Cowardice & FEAR – & J-La on the Perils of a Poker Fac*e

With thirty waterfalls on the Circuit du Sixt alone, it was only a matter of time before we did actually get to one.

Our first waterfall came in the form of lovely, summer, mountain rain; pitter-pattering on the roof of the caravan. It was only our third wet day since we left the UK, nearly two months ago. It was wonderfully refreshing!

I have my own interpretation of Mr Mercury's stirring anthem "We are the Campers." Freddie's home island of Zanzibar has not one but two rainy seasons, so it would not surprise me if his early camping days resembled ours – ALWAYS in the rain.

And that was why, having paid our dues, we had bought a caravan.

Part of the joy of the rain was having en-suite facilities, a kettle and a TV. We were nice and warm – and DRY in our tin box. The temperature had plummeted to 3°C last night, so we were feeling a little superior in comfort to the beardy mountain folk in their tents. The abundance of crusties did mean that there was no queue for showers, though. At least, that's what I thought...

We stopped short of singing in the rain but went for a wander up the Piste des Cascades, a 14km ski run down which we have skidded a number of times. It was lovely to see the cascades for which it was named, but it is graded as a blue run.

Marvel, up which we had walked the other day, is a green piste, the lowest grading for gradient - and that was hard enough! Before we ran out of puff and turned back, we did get some moody views of the Haut Giffre, with shrouds of mist, like feather boas, draped casually over the shoulders of the mossy green mountainsides.

As we drove down to the pretty town of Samoëns for lunch, the river was smoking as the hot sun made an appearance. We peered longingly in the window of our favourite patisserie but remained strong. We may have walked up a blue run – but we had still not burned off enough calories to enter!

We returned to the caravan for a coffee and a sleep, watching the mountains move in and out of view through our skylights as the mists came and went.

Travel is all about new experiences and today, I nearly got a black eye from a shower.

The lower shower block on the campsite was newly refurbished, but the upper shower block was altogether a bit rough and ready. Adjacent to the shower head was a chain to release the water, a bit like a high-level flush on a Victorian toilet. A flimsy nail was provided to keep the chain out of the way while you were showering. Needless to say, the chain, which was quite heavy, pulled out the nail mid-shower and the cast iron handle on the end of the chain socked me right in the eye! Maybe the prevalence of crusty mountain types was not the explanation for why there was no queue here for the shower. This shower HURT!

Having checked out the Tines on Tuesday, we went back on Wednesday to once again start our walk to the waterfall Cascade du Rouget.

Although we were above 1000m in altitude, the daytime temperature was still in the mid-30°s. Thankfully, much of the ascent was through shady forest. Cascade du Rouget, one of largest waterfalls in the area, is also known as "The Queen of the Alps". 80m of tumbling waters created their own cooling breeze and the Queen's fine spray misted our skin. It was bliss.

We decided to continue with the cooling theme on the way down and took the plunge in a mountain stream. On entering, the water was so cold that it felt like someone had whacked you across the shins with a plank!

During one of his Irish Wave Clinics, my windsurf instructor, Peter Hart, told me that I needed to show my feelings more. This came about because my serene smile did not reveal that I was TERRIFIED of the motorhome-sized waves that were breaking over my head each time I attempted to ride on their faces. On the photos of our mountain dip, the beatific smile of my "It is so cold it HURTS!" face was identical to the "I'm so scared I want to vomit!" face about which Peter had complained so Hartily!

We descended from the Cascade past someone wearing a T-shirt stating that "Fear leads to Cowardice". I stand with Yoda on the subject of fear. "Path to The Dark Side fear is; fear leads to anger; anger leads to hate; hate leads to suffering." And according to Yoda "Cowards are those who follow The Dark Side" - so the logic did stand up.

Very much in touch with The Force we were feeling.

Endured shower-based pain and cold water suffering we had. And even in Gigantic Irish waves, avoid fear and anger we did.

Stay on the Light Side, we will!

This was just as well. Our time in the mountains had come to an end.

We were about to begin our return journey back across France. Our next stop? Unlucky Al-levard!

18

UNLUCKY AL-LEVARD!

Slips, Trips & Falls; Mud, Misdirection & Missing Millions – &
Some Rude-Sounding Place Names!

It was an impressive drive from Sixt-Fer-à-Cheval to Alle-vard les Bains. We descended past the foot of Mont Blanc, then climbed back up through the ski resort of Megève, skirting the Bauges Regional Natural Park.

Being a complete child, however, my favourite landmark was Bastard Automobiles in Sallanches. Sadly, much like when I saw a bus in Zimbabwe with "Wankie Express" emblazoned down its side, I was just not quick enough with the camera to capture the moment on film.

Unfortunately, Zimbabwe has now rendered unremarkable the Safari Park, its associated buses and all things Wankie (even the Wankie Colliery Company Ltd!) by renaming it all "Hwange". Spoilsports. But if you want to get your car serviced by a real Bastard, Sallanches is still the place for you!

The other impressive thing about the drive was the

wrong turn in Albertville. The Sat Nav was a little slow updating itself on a junction. This rapidly necessitated an impressive multi-point turn on a narrow, mountain road. Mark made use of a kind but unsuspecting person's parking spot while I directed traffic, while ensuring that Big Blue didn't plummet over a precipice with Kismet in tow. Once again, I was in awe of Mr L's pin-point accurate reversing skills. I was beginning to have faith in our decision to forgo a motor mover!

Camping Clair Matin in Allevard was one of the loveliest, friendliest campsites at which we have ever stayed. Christophe welcomed us like long-lost family, before showing us around the beautifully kept, landscaped and terraced site on a little electric golf buggy. He recommended the nicest pitches as he went and even offered to bring us a table and chairs so that we could eat outside if we wanted.

Once we were settled, I discovered that the electric fused every time that I used the microwave. At reception, I accidentally interrupted Pascale during his dinner, but despite my protests, he came straight away to re-connect us. "Can I use the microwave on this hook-up?" I asked him. With a sideways look that said "Experience would suggest not" he answered "Non!" His shrug and wry grin possibly indicating an inner monologue along the lines of "What a stupid question!"

As he walked jauntily towards the caravan, Pascale grabbed my arm and started humming "Here comes the Bride", telling fellow campers delightedly "Je vais pour un Soirée sans électricité! - I am going for a Soirée without electricity!"

Sunday. It was not even 10am and I had already had cause to call him a word connected with an Automobile

Dealership in Sallanches! He mocked me for failing to find the Carrefour supermarket. Admittedly, it was not difficult to find. The route to the Carrefour consisted of just three turns: right out of the campsite; first left at the bottom of the hill; then first right into the Carrefour.

However, there were mitigating circumstances. As I approached the third right turn, I panicked. I was beckoned by a sign yelling "Casino – Parking'".

Now, Casino is another French supermarket chain. And it begins with C. So being beckoned by it was an easy mish-tayke that ANYONE could have made! I only realised that it was parking for an actual betting Casino once I was inextricably embroiled in The One Way System. I rationalised that it was nice to see a bit of the town as I drove around the whole of Allevard to get back to the Carrefour, located as it was, just yards from the campsite.

It turned out to be a bad day. I owed a long-standing gambling debt of £1m to Mark. (That's how SURE I was that Jack Nicholson starred in "Silence of the Lambs" – well, he often plays mad people and does look a bit like Anthony Hopkins... Don't you think?) An irresistible chance presented itself for me to equalise my debt. During our walk, I had bet Mark £1m that the Scottish Munros are mountains over 4000ft. I was so cocky and confident of my craggy credentials that I goaded him; "I *grew up* climbing. You shouldn't take ME on over mountain matters..." Surrounded by lofty peaks, I was forgetting two things. 1. How puny British mountains are, even though The Ben (Ben Nevis) is over 4000ft and 2. How hopeless I am with numbers.

Munros are only 3000ft. PAH! So I owed him £2m.

Then I stood on a dead bird when Mark said (and I

quote) "There are ACRES of clear pavement around. You're like "Unlucky Alf" in "The Fast Show!""

"Can't you just be satisfied?!" I spluttered indignantly. "You have mocked me, won £1m from me when I WAS SO SURE and now you're comparing me to Unlucky Alf!"

In moving from Sixt to Allevard, we had descended to around 500m. The temperatures were still in the Mid 30°s - but now had 40% humidity to add to the misery! It was too hot to do anything – at one point, Rosie nearly keeled over with heat exhaustion. Luckily, we were walking around the nearby lake at the time and could dunk her in the water to cool her off.

The bad news was that Mark tweaked his back and my shoulder came out in sympathy. The good news was that we were in a spa town awash with healing waters and replete with osteopaths! However, neither of us was too keen on braving thermal waters in the 30°C heat.

Fortunately, Monday brought a cooler 26°C with a slight breeze. What a relief! We did manage to go for a stroll – even though it seemed difficult to find walks in the area. The path that we followed boasted all sorts of signs along the way, exalting in the joys of being in nature. There were even lines of string on which walkers could hang handwritten messages to describe their feelings about being surrounded by the glories of creation. The route was spectacular; it granted us unrivalled views of a retail park, including a large pharmacy and a Lidl (we couldn't quite make out the neon sign announcing the petrol prices, which was a bit annoying since we needed to fill up) – and ended abruptly at the town's iron works!

The previous evening, we had tried to follow some of the yellow waymark signs. None of them seemed to go anywhere – the paths just petered out. We stumbled into one of those dark and spooky forests that appear in horror films, causing you to ask yourself "Why on EARTH would ANYONE IN THEIR RIGHT MINDS venture into THERE?!"

A lady had told us that the route that we were following led to a village, but there was no sign of civilisation and any residents would have needed some serious 4×4 machinery to get up that road to their houses. On the way back, we did stop briefly in Allevard les Bains and had a little wander around the town. It was very picturesque and there were some more yellow signs indicating walks from the centre, but I remain sure that they too led nowhere!

They say that trouble comes in threes. On our previous walk around the lake, Rosie had overheated and nearly keeled over. On our final night's lakeside wander, we lost Ruby. "She's down there on the shore." Mark said, unconcerned but when I went down the steep, shale bank in my trusty flip flops, there was no sign of her.

Never one to over-react, I flew straight into a panic. "What if she has been swallowed by a giant pike? Or sucked out of the reservoir by the pump for the hydro-electric scheme?" As it happened, she had simply lost track of how far she had run along the shore and some people on the far side whistled to us to let us know that she had come up the bank next to them.

Then we found a place with easier access to the lake for our water babies to immerse themselves. We went down through the trees but the mud on the shoreline was like glass. Mark, after telling me to be careful, slipped and went head over heels. Bearing in mind his bad back, I was distraught. Luckily, it didn't seem to affect his back too badly, but it was rather ironic that we hadn't worn clothes for days because it had been too hot and now, his clean T-shirt and shorts were covered in revolting, sticky mud.

And that, dear reader, is why we christened it Unlucky Al-levard!

19

A TRIP DOWN MEMORY LANE

Merths & Memories in Marsanne & Mirmande!

Once again, the sleepless nights proved redundant. It could have been so different... but it was unexpectedly a no-tears exit from our pitch at Allevarde. No-one had parked next to us – so instead of wondering how the heck we were going to get down a steep bank it was straight out across the two adjacent pitches and merrily on our way!

We followed the glacial blue River Isère as we meandered down through the mountains. The steep-sided valleys widened, until they were able to cocoon Grenoble in a soaring, green amphitheatre, crowned with a halo of bright, white limestone.

We knew immediately that we had entered a city. Pedestrians in suits rushed along pavements with phones glued to their ears. Impatient drivers cut in front of us or hooted impatiently when we didn't move forward to block the intersections completely with our caravan, even though doing so would only add further to the gridlock, chaos and frustration!

The last time that I had been in this area was on my 31st birthday – I was single then and had treated myself to "The Ultimate Adrenaline Weekend". Over the course of the weekend, I had done the highest bungee jump in Europe from Le Pont de Ponsonnas (103m). I had achieved 100km/h and pulled 2G on the Olympic Bobsleigh Run at La Plagne, in a racing bob with a professional driver and brake man (trying not to think about John Noakes overturning his bob on the Cresta Run!) Then a skidoo safari – swift and serpentine with bothersome bends (skidoos are not nimble at cornering and there were sheer drops to consider.) The Grand Finale had been a Mountain Bike descent, which was probably the scariest experience of the lot. During the build-up, the words "Last time I did this, I went over the handlebars seven times!" were uttered.

Suffice to say that I had a Hurtling Happy Birthday – and thankfully avoided the Hurt!

As the Isère flowed down to join the Rhône, we drove through the Vercors National Park past miles of regimented stands of shady, lollipop-shaped walnut trees. I had been previously unaware that the area has its own geographic Appellation for walnuts!

I took over at the wheel in St Romans, where we stopped for coffee and a cake at a lovely little drive-in boulangerie by the side of the road. We continued through St Nazaire en Royens, which had a stunning viaduct. The countryside felt alive – green and verdant, with everything growing fervently to make the most of the blistering summer sunshine.

The approach to Marsanne wound around a small, bosomy hill. It seemed to find favour with flocks of aspiring Niki Laudas, who raced down the opposite way on narrow hairpins. I guess that the sheer drops just added to the thrill. No stranger to adrenaline myself, I kept a cool head. We arrived safely and then imposed upon ourselves the challenge of getting on to Pitch 30, at the very top of a steep hill. This time, we had obeyed Caravan Confucius and scoped the site. Pitch 30 would not be the easiest to access, but it had the best views!

The proprietress was not sure that we'd make it up to Pitch 30 without a 4×4, but her hubby wasn't on hand to advise - and Mark had that look in his eye. The climb up the 1:3 hill was fine. The final reverse; uphill on gravel into the pitch was a little more touch and go. There was a puff of smoke and a distinct smell of burning from Big Blue – "her engine's working hard!" Mark said – but the only option was to line her up, put the pedal to the metal - and hope for the best!

The required manoeuvre was a full-speed, dog-leg reverse avoiding trees and the electric hook-up post. We were seriously worried about Big Blue's clutch but as we were coming to the end of our mountain stint, we were hoping that it might just see us home.

"Into Marsanne and up to Mirmande." The lady at reception directed me to find some nice dog walks. "Do you want me to write down the name 'Mirmande'?" "It's OK" I replied. "My husband knows it... He worked there thirty years ago. Picking cherries!"

So it was a trip down memory lane for both of us. It was always a long shot, but Mark was seeking the spot on the Rhône where he, Greg and Jackie*, his travelling companions, took a photo of themselves taking a bath in the river. They were travelling in an old Ford Transit van (not even a converted Transit van) which had rather fewer facilities than our caravan. There was also the quarry to track down, which was where they had camped for the few months that they had stayed in the area.

I think it is worth sharing here that Mark ran into Jackie, his erstwhile travelling companion, on one of our visits home. Although we had never met, I immediately knew that it was Jackie. Which was lucky, since Mark had his arms folded uncomfortably across his chest and didn't introduce us.

"I had one of those 'tumbleweed moments'" he explained later. "My mind went completely blank and I couldn't remember her name..." I almost collapsed with laughter. I could understand it if she was called Aoibheann or something, but you think 'Jackie' might be memorable. You know, since she shared the same name as his wife!

Our campsite, Les Bastets was lovely, on the side of a hill with far-reaching views across the plain to the mountains. There were black and white moths everywhere (French moths always makes me think of Inspector Clouseau – he would definitely pronounce it "Merths".)

Apparently, it was just "that time of year". The lady at reception said "they are not very interesting" but I thought that they were really pretty, all fluttering around like vast flurries of autumn leaves. I did wonder whether their appeal might wane later when we were trying to sleep in a caravan that resembled the butterfly house at Syon Park!

They say that insect protein is the future for feeding the world. Many moths seemed to perish in the dogs' water bowl, but this wasn't a problem. Rosie found them delicious and hoovered up the lot.

It had been cloudy as we left the mountains near Allevarde but we were back to cloudless, bluebird skies in the Drôme. The outlook had become a bit more Mediterranean. We had left behind the lush, green hills and distinctive Alpine chalets and were now in slightly more parched, stone villa and Cyprus territory. It looked a bit like Tuscany.

We had avoided using toll roads and with the van

windows open, the scent of pine and sage drifted in. There seemed to be no livestock. It was very much a growers' paradise; melons, peaches and apricots, plus fields of maize and sunflowers. The sunflowers were now fading and bowing their heads, as if ashamed of their lost beauty.

Luckily, there was a stiff breeze on the top of our hill, or the heat would have been unbearable. Following a quick and unsuccessful quarry-search around Mirmande, we took the doggies for a walk on the top of the Col which divided the valleys. Although it was 8pm, the temperature was still 28°C. There was no direct shade on our pitch. It was going to be a hot couple of days.

As night fell, it all became very Alfred Hitchcock. Swarms of moths were drubbing on the outside of the caravan. It sounded like a hailstorm. It was the second sinister sound of the day – the blades of the distant windmills on the Col when we walked there had sounded like the beating wings of the fiendish, dragon-like Nazgûl in the "Lord of the Rings" films.

We had to shut the caravan windows from the outside, keeping the insect nets closed on the inside to stop the moths from flocking into our living space. When Mark opened the door to take the dogs out, clouds of moths wafted in. It reminded me of our second honeymoon in Costa Rica. There, we had also spent a romantic evening trying to eliminate a plague of insects from our accommodation. However, our sojourn at Playa Zancudo (Mosquito Beach – yes really!) during Honeymoon II – The Sequel had deadly snakes in the mix, making it considerably more terrifying and uncomfortable than Moth Mount. We went to sleep to the deafening song not just of crickets, but of stridently stridulating cicadas.

I asked the lady in reception where would be a good

place to get down to the River Rhône for the dogs to swim. She said she was new to the area and didn't know. I told her that we would investigate and report back. We went to the Rhône and found nothing but factories and a large cooling tower. When I filed my report and told her that it was 'Horrible!' She expressed no surprise. "The Rhône is well known for its Nuclear Industry," she said. Why, thank you for letting us know!

We did, however, go up the River Drôme valley past Crest, which has one of the tallest castle keeps in France. It is 52 metres high and dates from the 12th Century. It is also pronounced 'Cray' which is why we didn't realise that it is where our friend's sister lives! We ended up in Aouste sur Sye, a beautiful, little town, where the pups had a welcome cool down in the water as we strolled along the banks of the river.

Then, finally, third day lucky, we did actually venture into Mirmande! The Tourist Office was just closing (it was 6pm) but we found a lovely café and since time had marched on, instead of having a coffee, we treated ourselves to a cold one. I nearly got mine for free, but unfortunately, we are too honest and told the waitress that she had missed it off the bill.

The Drôme is famous for its medieval hill villages; sentries from distant and more troubled times when a clear lookout was essential to survival. The golden stone houses of Mirmande seem to rush up the hill, with just a few buildings having the momentum to reach the summit, which is crowned with a fine castle keep and Cyprus trees.

First mentioned in 1187, Mirmande has risen like a stone phoenix from its own rubble a number of times. Incongruously, in the 19th century it was a silk town, in which three thousand people made their living spinning and working with silk. The village was gradually abandoned as the industry declined and the town fell into ruin. Then in 1926, the cubist painter and writer André Lhote founded a painting academy. Many artists took up residence and helped with the renovation.

Today, Mirmande is listed as a Historical Monument and, like Sixt-Fer-à-Cheval, is one of "the Most Beautiful Villages in France".

And having finally got there and seen it, I can't say that I disagree!

20

HAPPY WITH OUR LOT AT THE RIVER CAFÉ

Barjac, Lozère (South Central France) – "The corner of S.W. France that the British haven't discovered."

1st September - in over 50 years, I have succeeded in doing it only a handful of times.

Since I was a little girl, I have tried to make "Rabbit. Rabbit. Rabbit." the very first thing that I say on the first day of the month.

It was two minutes to midnight; "Not the 9 O'Clock News" had just finished. The final frame was a clock; which reminded me...

Mark was taunting me, trying to make me speak. I remained strong. Then I did it! "Rabbit. Rabbit. Rabbit." I enunciated proudly, the moment that midnight struck.

I was just explaining to Mark that it brings good luck as I turned and knocked over a full glass of water, which soaked the seats and all four dogs. Mark, of course, was inconsolable with mirth. I was not sure that this was a good portent.

Happy September!

We were moving from Marsanne to Barjac – and the first challenge was simply to get Kismet off Pitch 30. It had been the most difficult pitch yet to get on, but therein lies an important caravan lesson. What goes on might not come off. At least, not the same way...

The exit strategy involved the descent of a different hill. It was very steep and gravelly with two hairpins at the bottom. "Are you sure you can get down that way?" I asked Mark. He replied honestly and succinctly; "No..."

The Germans showed plenty of interest as they drove past; we were stuck on the second hairpin at the time. We managed to avoid any damage to Kismet's tail only by pressing into action the emergency shovel and digging out part of a bank and a rockery to allow the caravan enough swing. Caravan Confucius say; "Man Moving Large Caravan Must be Able to Swing Freely Both Ways!"

We broke the shovel, but once we had escaped the campsite, our route took us through the pretty hills to Montelimar, which I had previously known only as one of my least favourite flavour options in a tin of Quality Street. I am more of an Orange girl (cream or cracknel) but we're not going as far as Provence... *(There is a city called Orange in the Vaucluse, in case you're unsure of my reference!)*

Needless to say, Montelimar boasts an enticing Museum of Nougat, but we didn't have time to stop. Much concentration was required as we wound through the narrow streets, avoiding height hazards, lorries and hairpins. We crossed the Rhône and immediately entered the Ardèche.

The climb through the Ardèche Monts was stunning. The architecture changed almost immediately. We exchanged the rambling Italianate stone villas with terracotta roof tiles for more compact houses with lovely, fish-scale slate roofs. The slates contained tiny chips of mica, which glistened in the sun. The villages nestled in pretty, floral clusters on hillsides that were otherwise clad in dark green forest. Crags stabbing accusingly at the blue sky were sometimes indistinguishable from the stark ruins of hilltop castles. Big Blue did brilliantly as she meandered her way up alongside the Ardèche river, almost to the source. We topped out at 1266m over the Col de la Chavade. As we crossed the summit, we were faced with the completely different landscape of the Val d'Allier laid out before us.

We descended to our proposed stop near Langogne, on Lac de Naussac. Our campsite, Les Terasses du Lac promised "lakeside pitches". Our windsurfing kit was almost crackling with excitement.

If lakeside means "half way up a hill with houses between you and the lake shore", then the description of the campsite was entirely accurate. The route to carry our kit to the water was a steep path through a field. A Dutch couple with boards and sails strewn around their motorhome advised me that my trusty flip flops would not be suitable footwear with which to navigate the path, even without the encumbrance of windsurfer to carry. It was an open, parched site with no character and no shade – and the temperature was still in the 30°s.

It was 2.30pm and we were both weighing up whether we should just pitch and relax or drive on to another campsite either locally or further afield. A longer trip today would mean a shorter trip another day!

Even the huge mosaic of a windsurfer on the floor of the reception at Les Terrasses was not enough to persuade us that we had come home. We opted to go on. Mark found a campsite in Barjac, on the banks of the River Lot. It was 90-minutes' drive, just past Mende, the capital of the

Lozère. Every time we had made the decision to move on, it had proved to be a good call. This seemed to be no exception. Langogne was one of the ugliest places that we had encountered, whereas continuing on past Mende, we entered an area that was a designated UNESCO World Heritage Site.

Our tribulations were not over, however. Following the Sat Nav to the Camping Le Clos des Peupliers, it took us to the wrong place, which was, of course, down a really narrow dead end. (A wrong turn is NEVER down a wide road with its own convenient turning circle!) The road was closed off for the school run, so the caravan was suddenly caught amid a maelstrom of manoeuvring mums.

We attracted quite a lot of attention. A mum-committee formed spontaneously to offer expert advice on our best plan of retreat. School mums advising on a procedure which involved the incomprehensible concept of reversing was never going to go well. I have so many happy memories of my morning commutes in London. It was great sport watching pairs of duelling Yummy Mummies in 4×4 stand-offs in the congested streets during rush hour. They were like fighting bulls. NOBODY was going to back down. Or back up. It was not really a matter of saving face. They simply couldn't do it!

"Turn round at that corner and you can drive straight back out!" was proffered as the preferred option from the mums. They simply could not conceive the possibility of reversing a 40ft vehicle for 100 yards, back the way that we had come. It wasn't a straight reverse either; there was a chicane to negotiate between a large hole in the road on one side and a protruding stone staircase on the other.

I am sure that I explained it in passable French. However, the mums seemed fundamentally incapable of accepting the concept that the car parked right on the apex of their corner rendered turning around there impossible.

An argument broke out. We directly defied the mums' advice. I think that they were so consumed with insisting to each other that the corner "is ze only way!" that they didn't notice as we retreated in reverse. Thankfully, Mark was ON FIRE with his pinpoint backward accuracy and neatly avoided both the hole in the road and the steps. At least if anyone had noticed our defiant retrogression, British Honour had remained intact.

We relaxed and felt a bit smug as we finally went the right way to the campsite, however it was short lived. We were utterly horrified to see that the campsite entrance was through two narrow bridges on a U-shaped bend. The numbers on the width and height signs intimated that Kismet would make it through with inches to spare. However, a quick scout of the route intimated that we may experience the exact corollary of how the numbers suggest that it is mathematically impossible for a bee to fly.

We left the wide towing mirrors on, just to make sure; with a lot of gesticulating, hope and gritted teeth, we made it through!

The site manageress was the first person on our entire trip to show any concern about our having four dogs. There was a bit of a commotion as we walked around the site to choose a pitch. A Brittany Spaniel pup and a Pomeranian initiated a bark-off with Les Quatre Cavapoos. With sixteen of them in total, you can guess who might have had the upper paw in that challenge...

Luckily, Madam's hubby intervened. "I love British!" he told us, beaming from ear to ear. He promptly rolled up his sleeve, proudly revealing his tattoo of the band Madness. "I LOVE Madness!" he added, rather unnecessarily.

He suggested that we pitched in a deserted part of the site that was technically closed. We had a whole section of the campsite completely to ourselves.

Suffice to say that we were very happy with our Lot. We were right on the banks of the River Lot, in soothing shade and with access to the water for our Hot Dogs to cool off. Mark cooked us potatoes, eggs and speck outside, over-looking the river. I can't claim that any wild-haired Hugh Fearnley-Whittingstall presided over our River Cottage Café. Mark had actually brushed his hair this morning – the first time in ten days. Never let it be said that we were letting our standards slip!

Once again, we were lulled to sleep by the gentle sound of the river. Unlike the strident stridulators in Marsanne, the cicadas here sounded more like a muted telephone ring tone. Even our butterflies had raised the bar on gorgeous-ness. They were tiny little ones, which looked like Chalk Hill Blues, but they were almost lilac in colour and irides-cent. Beautiful!

There are four distinct types of landscape in the Lozère; basalt in the North East, the Aubrac Plateau, which has its very own breed of cattle; Granite in the mountainous Marg-eride; Limestone with glorious gorges in the Lot Valley; while Shale and Granite spell out the spectacular Cevennes National Park.

There is certainly A Lot to do here, but if you were to ask us what we did, our answer would be a bit Paul Daniels; "Not A Lot!"

We just took it easy in the ever-so-welcome shade, although the dogs did tire themselves out. In our splendid isolation, we could leave them off their leads to spend their days chasing around. They splashed in and out of the river and played with Gonzo, the site mountain dog, who more or less became The Fifth Man.

Living this life, even jobs are more fun. Doing our laundry in such a beautiful setting and relaxing by the river in between loads really didn't feel like a chore.

What more do you need when you've got The Lot?

21

TAKING IT EASY IN LES EYZIES

A Dazzling Dalliance in the Dordogne.

5th **September** - We seemed to be oscillating backwards and forwards through time.

From the Lozère, we went from Gallo Roman, via Celtic to Prehistoric at our destination on the River Vézère, a tributary of the Dordogne.

Summer also changed to Autumn as we drove through the Parc Naturel Regional des Causses. Deciduous trees surrounded the parched, golden fields with borders of blood-red foliage. Neolithic Dolmens and Menhirs (standing stones) abounded. It was a complete change from the dark, secret forests of conifers that we had recently left behind.

Summer re-joined us as we crossed into the Dordogne. Temperatures soared once again into the 30°s, while lush, green woodland clung to cave-ridden limestone escarpments above the river.

We decided that La Belle France really does deserve her title. Even the ordinary bits between the many celebrated tourist destinations are beautiful. We stopped at a motorway services at Severac le Chateau and were treated to views to die for over a hilltop village topped off with a chateau! Every village seemed to look like a film set – and here in the Dordogne, we were about to discover that a good few of them were.

France certainly is "the middle of nowhere", though. We meandered for miles without seeing any large towns and wondered at what drives the economy, other than EU grants. We saw plenty of evidence of EU support in the fabulously engineered new roads. We saw a spectacular viaduct which spanned an entire valley. It led from, well, nowhere much to nowhere much! Mark said that he had found only seventeen major cities marked in bold in our atlas of France. Two of these were Caen and Poitiers, neither of which would warrant the title "seething metropolis" in my book.

We followed the Dordogne River to Sarlat-la-Canéda. Then we rocked up at Les Eyzies-de-Tayac, which was just gorgeous. We were, once again, back in limestone country. There is a rich history of prehistoric man in the area – the caves here had been used as troglodyte dwellings for thousands of years. Magnificent friezes of prehistoric paintings were discovered by a group of schoolboys in the Lascaux Cave during the 1940s. However, like most of the most really stunning places it was very touristy. We came across more Brits here than at any other time during our travels.

The town of Les Eyzies, right on the River Vézère, is backed by an overhanging limestone cliff, into which some of the buildings nestle. Personally, I would feel uncomfortable with that tonnage of stone hanging over my head, but I suppose that it had been there for millennia! The town had the feel of the Cotswolds; that aching but over-commercialised prettiness of Broadway or Bourton-on-the-Water, down even to the golden Cotswold-type stone.

After a long drive, we felt that we had earned a relaxing glass of wine. Mark nipped out and in the absence of a supermarket, stopped in an artisan cave. He returned with a box containing six bottles of local Bergerac wines. While Bergerac does not share quite the kudos of the Grand Vins of neighbouring Bordeaux, the bottle that we opened was by FAR the most expensive that we have bought on the trip – but it was so worth it.

It cost €6!

I am not very knowledgeable about French wines. To be honest, for many years I studiously avoided them (and all things French) on principle, since the French banned British beef due to Mad Cow Disease. This was, of course, before the French admitted that not only did they have Mad Cow Disease – they had been nourishing their cows on dried sewage for years!

In the UK, French wines are also about twice the price for half the quality of the New World wines, which are, after all, made from French grapes from French vines exported out there, often with a French wine maker in tow. In fact, after The Great French Wine Blight, many French vineyards were re-planted with French vines from the USA!

Anyway, I shall get off me soapbox and stop wining.

We relaxed with an evening walk down by the river. The pups loved it. It was so picturesque with the sunset lighting up Les Eyzies and the cliffs above. The campsite, La Rivière was beautiful and tranquil - and thank goodness, we had a shady spot. Sadly, it was fully booked at the weekend, but we decided that from here, we might go on to the seaside and leave Steve in peace.

Steve was the reason that we had come to Les Eyzies; in

fact Steve is largely the reason that we accidentally bought a caravan and chose this lifestyle! He had joined us to give help and moral support on our Maiden Voyage and had left Britain at about the same time as us to move here with his wife. He looked well and said that already, after two months, he couldn't imagine living back in the UK with all the traffic and the cold, grey weather.

We met with Steve in Sarlat. Steve has a particular talent for giving directions. He hit his own personal zenith of vagueness the last time we saw him with "I'll see you at the pub. I can't remember the name of the pub or the name of the village..." I won't go into the lengthy shenanigans involved in THAT particular rendezvous. Suffice to say that it wasn't first left, first right and as such, we really COULD miss it. To add to the interest, the pub was in a mobile phone black spot. Ultimately, the achievement of togetherness for pie and a pint did involve the dispatch of a search party!

So when Steve said; "I'll meet you at the Lidl on the road to Bergerac" we at least had some place names to run with, although we did find that in this area, ALL roads lead to Bergerac. Steve added a further element of jeopardy by altering the arrangements from "See you there at 12" with a phone call at 11.15 to say "let's meet at 11.30!"

We found him eventually, a little late after sitting in horrendous traffic. Traffic – maybe. But definitely no cold, grey weather. Mark had called Steve to let him know that we were running late "We're just on the outskirts of Bergerac, so where is the Lidl?" "You're WHERE?!!!!" Later, Steve berated us at the wind up; "You had me going there..."

Sarlat is a beautiful, medieval city and is apparently where they filmed Les Miserables. It was market day, so it was really busy and a bit much for the dogs in the 36°C heat.

Our Furbies were a bit freaked by the crowds and getting barged by shopping bags. They are only tiny, after all. Mark and I found it quite tricky trying to carry all four of them, one under each arm!

Steve tipped us off that they filmed Chocolat in nearby Beynac, so that had to be done. Beynac is on the Dordogne river, so we figured that a doggy swim would also be in order. Beynac was much less crowded and was utterly beautiful. We had a delicious fruit ice cream in the shade looking up at the ramparts of the castle - and the pooches did indeed get their swim.

We met up with Steve again in the evening for a drink at his new house, which was as amazing as the surroundings. Steve had shown us pictures before he moved. The house itself looked spectacular, but the photos had not prepared us for the setting! It overlooked nothing but rolling hills and forest. We sat on the terrace in the warm evening and enjoyed the bottle of Bergerac that we had brought as a house warming present. The only thing that spoiled the ambience was the dogs raising a frantic cacophony because we had to leave them out of sight of Steve's pet rabbits – which distressingly for them happened to be out of sight of us. I guess that you can't have everything!

We all had dinner in the excellent Restaurant les Combarelles. The proprietor, Didier, had agreed that it was OK to bring dogs, but was perhaps a little taken aback when we rocked up with four.

We ate outside in the balmy evening air and I must admit, for a set menu costing €20, I have rarely tasted better food. I had scallop kebabs to start followed by Magret of Duck – slices of rare duck with crispy, bacon-flavoured skin in a creamy peppercorn sauce, served with a timbale of root vegetables. I can still taste it now! Pink slices of duck melting on my tongue. I had a small, local baked cheese roundel with honey and walnuts to finish. Mark had a cassoulet and sticky toffee pudding. We are on a budget, so we don't eat out often. It really was a treat and so lovely to share it with our dear friend who, like us, was starting a new life. We raised a toast to Living our Dreams!

As with so many of the buildings in the area, the restaurant was built into a cave in the cliff. Didier explained to us that the farmers all used to help each other with building. They would put wedges of wood into cracks in the rock during the winter. These would expand as they got wet or froze. This would break off pieces of stone. When they had amassed enough loose stone, they would build. I am not sure if it is strictly the freeze-thaw process, but I might allow it as that so that I can mention it!

The freeze-thaw process is something that I learned about at school. Water seeps into cracks in rocks, expands as it freezes and thus breaks up the rock. I have seen it in action only once – and remarkably, this was not in the mountains. Rather, it was in the Mad House where we used to live – and about which I will probably write one day – since it was an experience that was frequently very much stranger than fiction!

During dinner with friends one evening, we heard a large crash. Following a couple of harsh winters, it appeared that the stone coping around our roof had given up its 400-year battle with gravity. Our dinner guests were slightly bemused by my reaction to the partial collapse of our home. I was overjoyed – I love science in action and it's not every day that you get to witness the freeze-thaw process first hand!

In the middle of the night, dear little Lani scratched at the caravan door to go out. It was a warm, clear night and the stars were truly beautiful. I could see the Milky Way like a diaphanous swag across the sky, while the cliffs of Les Eyzies were illuminated, making it look like a fairy-tale city. Although Lani got me up no less than three times to go out in the night and I felt like a zombie, I was still really pleased to have witnessed such a magical spectacle.

We were disappointed that we couldn't stay longer. The campsite had a special offer of 7 nights for the price of 6, but was fully booked at the weekend. We had paid only €15 per night for the three nights that we had stayed. It was one of the cheapest sites yet – and certainly one of the best.

It was raining lightly the following morning, which was an incredible relief after the relentless heat. We walked the dogs on the river and prepared to move on.

We elected to head for the coast. We can't deny that we were really rather excited about the prospect. The pups had experienced plenty of culture. They were also ready to get back to the seaside!

22

ISLAND LIFE – BOYARDVILLE, ÎLE D'OLÉRON

A Storm in a Teacup; The Ubiquitous Evil & The Wrong Kind of Wind!

8th September - The dogs were suddenly excited. Even we were aware of the delicious, briny smell of the sea as we crossed the bridge on to the Île d'Oléron. At 22 miles long, Île d'Oléron is France's second largest island after Corsica. There is no toll on the bridge; Oléron is altogether more down-to-earth than its swanky neighbour, Île de Ré.

With salt-pans and mussel beds on each side of the road, we were overjoyed to see the gorgeous, big, blue expanse of the Atlantic spread out before us.

We mused that this trip had been the longest period that we had spent away from the ocean since we took up *("became obsessed with")* windsurfing.

The run over to Oléron was probably one of the most ordinary journeys of the trip so far, although with this being La Belle France, the countryside would still rank as "quite pretty"! The rain cleared by 11.30 as we departed the Dordogne to enter the white, limestone villages and vineyards of Bordeaux. The vineyards were like works of art. Each vine was perfect; pruned exactly to match its neighbour. The lines were completely straight and fastidiously weeded. A mere glimpse of these vines would make it obvious to anyone that the wines of Bordeaux were a cut above.

Still, travel is always an adventure and the Sat Nav decided to add interest to the journey to fill in for where the landscape was lacking.

Initially, it was our fault; we forgot to set the Sat Nav to "Avoid Toll ways" and in no time, we had racked up €16 in tolls, the cost of a night's camping! Swiftly relieved of €10 for coffee and a cake and we hastily adjusted it to "Quickest Route" although the Sat Nav algorithms seemed to defy the laws of mathematics and geometry. A red 'A' road rocketing straight up the hypotenuse of a triangle from "You Are Here" to "Île d'Oléron" leapt out at us from the map. Yet the Sat Nav opted for "Quickest Route" via a meandering series of unmarked roads, through the middle of absolute nowhere.

It turned out to be the towing equivalent of a steeplechase. During my stint at the wheel, I had to navigate narrow roads, hairpins, bollards and chicanes, many of which bore the evidence of less careful drivers scraping the sides. The pièce de résistance, however, was an excursion the wrong way down a short one-way street, which vomited us out onto a major roundabout.

The locals very generously stopped in their hordes to wave their arms and point out how stupid I was, but even in the face of such censure, there was no way that I was reversing back. Thankfully, a very kind lorry took pity on the Damson in Distress and held up traffic on the roundabout to allow me to pull out. Even this was not a straightforward manoeuvre; it was quite a sharp turn, but whoever you are, Thank You. You are a gentleman and Knight of the Road, who appreciates that foreigners on unfamiliar roads do make genuine mistakes. And to all the rest of you, we promise to cut you some slack and afford you the same courtesy should the same ever happen to you in England!

Our campsite Les Saumonards at Boyardville was magnificent – in the midst of a forest, shaded by tall pine trees and offering a pitch right next to the walk through to the beach. It has a wonderful, peaceful ambience. We were really excited and looking forward to our stay.

We treated ourselves to a beautiful walk on the beach to shake off the trials of the trail. The golden, evening light lit up Fort Boyard, the Napoleonic ocean fort in the bay and highlighted the pretty town of La Rochelle, clinging to the mainland. Our Fur Babies were absolutely thrilled. Having been brought up in Bournemouth, the beach is their natural element.

We met a really sweet couple; the hubby told me that I was the loveliest English person that he had ever met and both he and his wife adored the dogs. They noted how well behaved and happy they were and very kindly commented that it was the home environment that made them so. Particularly following such a stressful drive, it was so uplifting to experience such open and spontaneous kindness!

Saturday came and I was in trouble again. We walked on the beach to have a look at one of the windsurfing bays. I took a photo of the beautiful sky. We got some looks. I did not realise until later that getting out my camera phone was a little insensitive; we had inadvertently strayed on to a naturist beach!

Mark cooked up some local Boyardville mussels that we

had bought in the Intermarché. They were truly delicious; so fresh and only €5. I have always been a fan of Mark's mussels... In combination with the garlic bread that he made, I think we will be safe from Vampires for a day or two – and our friends in the UK will probably be glad that we won't be home for a couple of weeks yet!

We met a lovely German couple, Friederike and Dieter and their gorgeous, black miniature poodle, Arturo. They kind of adopted us and one evening, we walked into Boyardville to dine with them. Five dogs in a restaurant. Must be a record! But France is like that. It is really dog friendly. We had the local speciality, which is, of course, moules frites (you can never have too many mussels!) They were delicious.

Friederike and Dieter wanted us to go around the island with them on Tuesday, but I am not sure that anyone other than a windsurfer would understand our reasons for declining. We had told them that we wanted to windsurf, which was fine with them, but when they bumped into us on Tuesday morning, the conversation went something like this;

"We thought that you were going windsurfing."

"We're waiting for the wind."

"But it is windy!"

"It's not enough wind. We need about 14 knots to get going. It's supposed to get up to 18 knots at 11 o'clock."

"It's nearly 11 o'clock now."

"Yes, but the wind hasn't quite come through yet. And it's in the wrong direction."

I don't think that they would have understood why, in the end, we didn't go windsurfing after all. The wind was not only a little feeble, but it was due to switch further in the wrong direction and a thunderstorm was forecast.

Being out on the sea clinging on to a five-metre tall carbon fibre lightning conductor (mast) is not a great strategy for survival. Is that enough excuses? I guess that we could have said that we're British - and it was just the wrong kind of wind!

In fact I'm not sure why we ever bother trying to go windsurfing. It is such a fickle sport.

Once we had completely abandoned the possibility of windsurfing, we decided to drive around the island ourselves to scope out the other potential windsurfing beaches for future reference. This did differ markedly from Friederike's objective, which had been to drive around the island, have a sumptuous lunch and visit a boutique!

Billboards around the island warned of impending 'Orages' (Storms). The Orages came that night with vengeance. I have never experienced anything so loud – the thunder shook the caravan and the rain was so torrential that it felt like we had stumbled on to a pitch beneath Niagara Falls. Poor Rosie was terrified. She was trembling uncontrollably and we couldn't even distract her with a treat, which was unprecedented. We opened the blinds to watch the sky lighting up. The trees showed up as stark, black silhouettes against dusky, mauve sheet lightning, with the odd magnesium-white bolt zig zagging like a rip through the other-worldly backdrop.

We had invited Friederike and Dieter over for a drink – unsurprisingly, they didn't brave the storm. Just as we were settling down to watch the second episode of "Longitude" on the computer (the storm had knocked out the electrics. The CD player sounded distorted and the TV wouldn't even come on.) they arrived. We had a lovely evening chatting with them. Arturo cuddled up to me for ages, which they said was highly unusual.

We discussed language and how it defines a state of mind. Anthropologists claim that it is not possible to really understand a culture without a command of the language – and it goes deeper than just deciphering poetry and folk-lore. Friederike said that she was learning Arabic, a language with no verbs! A very different view point to Europe where "doing" kind of characterises us. I was fasci-nated and it made me want to learn Arabic too, since my European perception simply couldn't understand how a language could possibly work without verbs.

Our iPod seems to have become predictive. It started playing "Thunder only Happens When It's Raining" followed by "Catch the Wind"; this might seem apt after our abortive windsurfing experience but the timing was even more impeccable because the latter track coincided, mid-cuddle, with Kai letting loose a dainty little botty burp into Mark's hand!

As our departure loomed, chaos was brewing in the caravan. I had a sleepless night worrying about towing the caravan off the Île in a storm. Reception had assured us that the bridge would close if there was too much wind, because "Caravans have been known to blow over..." Well that had really reassured me! However, we woke to a beautiful morn-ing. I saw Friederike as we checked out. Bless her, she shed a tear and said that she was worried that she would never see us again. We exchanged hugs, details and open invitations to visit.

But a very British storm was brewing – or not brewing – which was more to the point. Our low-voltage caravan kettle had mutinied – it had started to switch itself on and off spontaneously. But worse than that, we're down to our last box of M&S "Gold" Tea Bags.

Fewer than one tea bag per day for the rest of the trip...

Would we re-use or simply accept our sentence? Could we face abstinence or would we be forced to survive our final few weeks subjected to the ubiquitous evil that is Lipton's Yellow Label – seemingly the only brand of tea that is ever available anywhere abroad?

23

HOLY FOOLS – ÎLE DE NOIRMOUTIER

In Search of The World's Most Expensive Potato; The Longest Submersible Road in Europe & The Perfect Storm.

14th September – We wondered if we had made a mistake leaving Oléron. As we departed the Charente Maritime for the Vendée, we drove through a featureless coastal plain to Longeville and a campsite recommended to us by Friederike and Dieter.

It was always a risk. Campsite Petit Rocher advertised that it would accept only one dog – which seemed to be a worrying standard on all of the campsites in this area. On our travels, most campsites had stipulated "maximum 2 dogs" although we had not yet encountered a problem checking in with four. In Longeville, however, even my "Ils son tres petit et tres gentile" made no difference. The one dog policy was politely, yet strictly enforced.

While the campsite looked pleasant, with lots of woodland and the beach nearby, it was quite commercial. We decided that we "Didn't want to stay there anyway..." – the sour grape rebuttal of the snubbed!

As always, however, it worked out better in the long run. It was early afternoon, so we decided to push on to one of our planned stops a couple of hours further up the coast. I love turning up at new places and exploring but it is a while since I had been this excited about arriving somewhere!

People come to Noirmoutier for many reasons. Some seek the world's most expensive potato, the Bonnotte "The Caviar of the Potato World"; others the longest submersible road in Europe "The Gois" (pack an inflatable boat – or you can always shin up one of the refuge markers to dodge the twice daily peril of being overwhelmed by the tide!) Then there are the delightful little whitewashed, terracotta-roofed houses with blue shutters; or the Black Friars, for whom the island is named and the inspiration behind the novel "Holy Fools" by Joanne Harris, author of "Chocolat".

Holy Fools are those who denounce worldly goods and deliberately flout society's conventions. We didn't do it for religious reasons - but if the cap fits...

The gentle climate for which Joanne Harris' grandparents moved to Noirmoutier on doctor's orders is also the reason behind Noirmoutier's nickname; "The Mimosa Isle".

We came for the windsurfing, however – and we struck gold!

Campsite Domaine le Midi was right at the centre of the sweeping, west-facing beach of Barbâtre. Windmills, always a good omen for a windsurfer, graced the shoreline to the north. We arrived in sunshine, with a steady 18 knots of south westerly breeze blowing on shore. Paradise! Unfortunately, we had the more pressing matter of getting the caravan pitched and set up. Otherwise, we would have been straight out.

We were in a part of the Vendée which boasts an attraction known as "Le Jardin du Vent"- "The Garden of the

Wind". Obviously, it is also famous for the Vendée Globe sailing competition. Other than the rather incongruous flying, killer squirrels, which seemed to feature on the advertising boards for the area, this looked like our kind of place.

The guy at reception was really sweet. As he checked us in, he said that normally, they only allow two dogs but he had seen that ours were "petit and gentile" – saving me even having to deploy my standard four-dog justification. He said that he would charge us only for one dog, which was brilliant, since dogs were usually charged at €4 each per night.

With the joy of arrival we felt a bit feckless and finished last night's bottle of wine. Then we opened another one. Always a mishtayke! I took a picture of the full moon and posted it on Facebook with the caption "I used to be a vampire but I'm cured Now-OOOOO." My friend Tim did comment that he thought I meant werewolf. That is the trouble with two bottles of Bergerac. You mis-spell werewolf slightly and people think that you wrote "vampire"!

Thursday came and wind was forecast. We rigged and launched but probably an hour too late. Apart from the lack of wind, my only complaint was the overcrowded beach. There was not a soul to be seen! Actually we had a lovely sail, despite both getting knocked down by a rather heavy shore break. I caught and rode a couple of the lovely, rolling waves. I emerged from the shore break with a rather flattering seaweed wig.

For most people, windsurfing is a sport that you try on holiday with no tuition and rubbish equipment. "I tried it once" we hear so often. "I couldn't get the sail up and I kept falling in!" The rewards are there if you persevere, however and windsurfing is the most exhilarating sport in which I have ever partaken. It is up there with skiing and riding a horse; you experience the edge of control while harnessing the surging dynamism of nature. An Arabian proverb states; "The wind of heaven is that which blows between a horse's ears." Windsurfing is much the same.

A windsurfing buddy, John, once told me "You always remember your first wave ride." I remember mine vividly. Windsurfing at Branksome Dene Chine near Bournemouth, I accidentally caught a large wave (or rather, it caught me!) I was hurled at high speed towards the shore and deposited in an ungainly heap on the beach. The only thought going through my brain at that point was "I have absolutely GOT to do that again!"

The Hawai'ian people view riding waves as a religious experience. The magical sensation of being propelled by the forces of nature down the face of a wave is hard to put into words. The best description that I can offer you is from an early description of a Hawai'ian surfer; "He is a Mercury... A brown Mercury. His heels are winged and in them is the swiftness of the sea."

Our German neighbour came to watch us on the water. He had told us that he used to windsurf. I doubt that these Holy Fools impressed him at all. With such light wind, I am not sure that our Mercurial heels offered the most breath taking demonstration of capturing the swiftness of the sea!

He and his wife were very understanding, however, when Rosie and Lani paid them an impromptu visit and ate all of his little dog's food! He was a really cute little dog – they told us that they had given him a home after they found him in a forest in Poland.

As Friday dawned, our Predictive iPod played "It's Raining Again". Why, thanks for letting us know! It did experiment with irony by following up with "Mr Blue Sky".

There was a bit more wind than forecast and it came

through a little sooner than expected. We were preparing for an early evening sail. We had a lazy morning but we felt the wind shaking the awning. It was time to get out there! We took the dogs to the beach; the iPod seemed to have moved from predictive to spookily accurate in the fore-telling; Mr Blue Sky did make an actual appearance.

The windsurfing conditions were challenging – it was getting towards high tide, so the shore break was ferocious, making it difficult to launch and it was fairly wavy once we got out the back. Considering that I hadn't windsurfed for a couple of months and hadn't ridden my small, strong-wind board since I don't know when, I was delighted. I made my gybe (downwind turn) out the back on the face of a wave and was still planing when I flipped the rig. (Planing is when the board starts to skim across the tops of the waves like a speed boat, a sensation that feels like you are flying. Planing out of a turn is the Holy Grail for a windsurfer!)

My windsurfing fitness left a bit to be desired and I had to land after each run to get my breath back. My gybes were mostly dry but when I dropped the odd one, it was difficult and extremely tiring to waterstart (get back on board) in the wind shadows in between the large waves.

We made the perennial mistake of those having way too much fun by opting to do "just one more run". Like the second bottle of wine, it is always a mishtayke because when you're just too tired, that one more run has a great propensity to result in injury!

By now, the wind had really got up. It was honking. I was hugely overpowered and my sail was constantly being ripped out of my hands. Then Mark got flattened by the shore break. The wind was so strong that he could easily have used my tiny sail but the wind caught his man-sized spinnaker and hauled him over the front. He bashed his rib on the hard, wishbone section of his boom. We both limped back to shore. I had a sore backside from being bounced on the sea bed beneath a wave and Mark had very bruised ribs. Nevertheless, it was a massive amount of fun and after a wind drought of nearly three-months we were beginning to feel like proper windsurfers again.

The doggies seemed fine. We had left them home alone for the first time in the caravan while we nipped out for our hour together on the water. When we were re-united, Ruby shouted at us for about ten minutes and refused even to come near us, never mind give us a cuddle. Little Lani couldn't get enough of us. She gave us an industrial licking and huge hugs. Kai was jumping around, wanting to play while Rosie just buggered off! She trotted back later, smelling of fish. I suspect that she might have taken advantage of our distraction to explore the special sinks that are provided here for the specific purpose of washing your cockles, mussels and other shell-bound booty of the popular French pastime "pêche à pied" or "fishing on foot".

On the Île d'Oléron, we had the wrong kind of wind. Here on Noirmoutier, we seemed to have found the perfect storm!

24

MORE ISLAND LIFE - ÎLE DE NOIRMOUTIER

Moulins, Malodorous Mongrels & Mission Mussel!

It was Saturday and we had planned to visit the town of Noirmoutier, but as I walked the dogs on the beach, there was an emergency.

A chap and his son were just launching their windsurfers. The son was a beginner, but the chap planed into the distance on his first reach. I raced back to the caravan. I had left Mark de-rigging our sails, because no more wind was forecast. Fortunately, in my short absence, he had only taken down yesterday's tiny sail, so I rushed straight back to the beach with my larger kit and had a cheeky, lovely hour on the water.

It is amazing how the Atlantic, which had punished both of us yesterday, was smooth, sun kissed and loving today. I didn't even get my hair wet as I glided round gybes and carved graceful 'S' shapes on little waves. I had to work for my reaches, as the wind was light but it was really beautiful when I got planing. I went miles out with every run. It was so much less tiring than yesterday - and so much less terrifying... Poor Mark decided that it was probably best to be cautious. He didn't think that he had broken a rib, but his chest was very sore and the pain seemed to have moved into his shoulder blade.

I so enjoy watching The Fab Four on the beach. Last night, Lani and Ruby went berserk, running miles as they chased flocks of birds along the shore line. This morning, seeing Rosie bound up the steps to the beach, oozing excitement was just lovely. She really is the embodiment of "joie de vivre." Rosie greets each new experience, however mundane, with nothing less than rapture!

The morning was not without conflict. An evil-looking chocolate lab (yes really!) chased our babies rather nastily. I grabbed its collar and frog marched it back to its owners; its front feet barely touching the ground. Mess with my Fur Babies and you mess with me. Its owners knew. I think the look in my eye dissuaded them from challenging me!

During our evening walk on the beach, the pups treated themselves to a free feast of decomposing Mermaid's purse. (A Mermaid's purse is a dog fish egg case). I had never smelled anything quite so evil. I couldn't even sit in the caravan with them because the smell made me retch!

We had planned to bathe them anyway, as they were all very salty and sandy. Kai was the worst olfactory offender. Even after his bath, his breath still smelt like he had the devil's doings lodged in the back of his throat. I tried feeding him some smelly sausage and a bit of Parmesan cheese, but he still stank like Satan's armpit. He would be sleeping with Mark that night! I was worried that our Belgian neighbour with the grey pony tail and matching handlebar moustache might be offended by my coughing and retching. I hoped that he wouldn't think that I was trying to impersonate him, since that was how he started each day...

Sunday kicked off with digging a German camper van out of the sand. It was a young couple with a baby. They had arrived on the island at 11pm, but all the campsites and Aires were closed or full. The poor things had spent the night in the car park. Then, having chosen their pitch, had promptly wheel spun their way to virtual burial in the sand.

They had not had breakfast so I offered them a hot drink and some croissants. I recommended the pitch opposite, recently vacated by a substantial motorhome, but I think the bloke was feeling a bit embarrassed. He wanted to take charge and do his own thing. They did pitch and set up there after a while, but then moved everything by hand to another pitch. It was away from us but closer to the beach, so I didn't take it personally!

We chortled to ourselves as to how we were now so experienced at caravanning that WE would never get our van stuck. Oh, how we would come to regret such unseemly pride, which inevitably comes before a whacking great fall.

Having bathed the malodorous mongrels, we decided that it would be nice to try to stay sand-free for at least 24-hours, so we drove off the island to go for a forest walk near Fromentine. Just as Mark and I stopped to discuss directions, the mutts did, of course, manage to find a nice stagnant pond to explore. Ah well, at least it was not sand - and nothing in the world could smell as bad as that Mermaid's purse!

The wind was conspicuous by its absence, so we kept making plans to go and see the windmills La Guérinière but never quite got it together. We wandered up there on a Wednesday evening - and were so glad that we hadn't set aside a whole day! The beach at Le Guérinière was covered with stinky seaweed and signs saying "No Dogs Allowed". The windmills were very sweet – they had been converted into houses. You have heard of "The Satellite of Love" - one was called "Le Moulin d'Amour – The Windmill of Love". We drove up to the forest just past La Guérinière, where we were able to give the doggies a run off their leads.

I am not a huge fan of sightseeing but I am nothing compared to Mark. "I'd like to go and see the town of Noirmoutier." "You've been to the Supermarket on the road to Noirmoutier, is that not close enough?" he replied... I am surprised that he didn't also postulate that a trip to the supermarket was WAY better than Sea World. Well, there are tanks of live lobster and crabs on the fish counter. What more could I want?

I eventually did get him to Noirmoutier, but only under the guise of "Mission Mussel"! We had stopped at the supermarket, but the fish counter had run out of mussels. HA! I couldn't have planned it better. There was no choice but to go on.

Noirmoutier was very quaint and we enjoyed walking around the narrow, cobbled streets, overlooked by the impressive, 12th century castle. We kept running into the same foursome with their little, white poodle. "Aw, isn't he CUTE!"; "Hi! Nice to see you again! Bye. Have a great day!"; "Oh Hi. Fancy seeing you AGAIN. Take care. Enjoy your trip!"; "We really must stop meeting like this..."

We scored a couple of kilos of mussels in a fishmonger's. They were so fresh that hardly any of them were closed. Mark deployed about half a pound of butter on his garlic bread and doubled the amount of garlic from the Vampire-repelling quantities used on Oléron. I hope the dogs realised that this was our revenge on them for that Mermaid's purse.

Our Anniversary present came a day early, which was lucky. The campsite was closing for the season on our actual

Anniversary, so we had to leave first thing. Fortunately, our Anniversary wind forecast also downgraded from 30kts to 15. It was a relief on two counts; we wouldn't be forced to miss a great windsurfing day - and we didn't fancy towing a large caravan over the bridge back to the mainland with the wind blowing Force 6!

There was always the second route off the island besides the bridge, although we were not sure that we were the perfect vehicular candidate for the Passage du Gois. The Gois features on the website "Dangerous Roads". It is an ancient causeway, which sinks beneath the waves twice a day. Mindful of the fate of the German couple who had been stuck in the sand, we didn't fancy getting Kismet and Big Blue embedded to await being swamped the incoming tide.

The wind was a little too southerly in the morning but it swung round in the early afternoon. There were a few kites on the water further down the beach and a lone windsurfer. We decided that it was time to get out there! My kit was rigged and ready, so I launched as the guinea pig. The tide was just on the turn and it was absolutely beautiful – smooth rolling waves to ride; joyous! I did a few reaches then came in and told Markie to get himself out there in case the wind dropped. We had a couple of short sessions each and just didn't want to stop.

We were shattered by the time we had de-rigged, washed sand off the kit and then packed up the caravan, ready for a swift exit tomorrow.

It was our final move of the trip - towards St Malo.

25

ST COULOMB – HEADING BACK HOME TO MR COCK UP!

"Success is stumbling from failure to failure with no loss of enthusiasm." – Winston Churchill

It was a long-ish drive from Noirmoutier to St Coulomb, near St Malo – the last stop on our French Odyssey.

It appeared that we had been getting a bit cocky with our caravan skills and it was time for the gods to hand us a leveller. Mark had nonchalantly swung Kismet in reverse on to our pitch at Barbâtre perfectly; first time. However, it looked as though we were going to end our trip exactly the way we began – on a colossal note of incompetence.

At the Camping les Chevrets, we set our hearts on a pitch with a gorgeous view through pine woods over the sea. There was a slight incline to get in the pitch; a few obstacles; not much manoeuvring room. We were experienced caravanners now, though. It was nothing we couldn't handle...

Manoeuvring such a large caravan, we did, of course, immediately attract an audience. Mesdames opposite, a collection of magnificently Reubenesque French ladies in floral, cotton dresses, came over to point out "Beaucoup de fumée!" – lots of smoke – billowing out of Big Blue's engine. The French couple next door looked worried. "You know our car is there?" they fussed. A concerned looking Dutch man was trying to retain his Low Country cool, casually reading a book, while keeping a discreet but beady eye on the rear corner of his motorhome.

Another French neighbour adopted a completely different tack. He cracked open a stubby and pulled up a pew.

We did the reverse in a series of three discrete and distinct cock ups; each accompanied by "Beaucoup de fumée!" – and the very real worry that our van, Big Blue, was suddenly going to burst into flames!

First, the back of the caravan narrowly missed grounding. We pulled forward to get into a better position, then reversed back again and caught the rear corner steadies. I think it was at this point that someone in our audience advised us that another person had tried but ultimately abandoned their attempt to get on to that pitch. Oh well, that was that.

The gauntlet was down. There was no way that we would allow ourselves to be thwarted now!

On the third attempt, something seemed to be dragging. I was watching the back of the caravan to ensure that we didn't ground out or catch the corner steadies again - while avoiding collision with the car and motorhome. I couldn't work out what the grinding noise was – until I noticed the deep furrow that was being ploughed by our grounded jockey wheel...

We wobbled back and forth in the small space available and eventually got the caravan on the pitch (yeah!) but still had to get her level and exactly line up the ALKO wheel lock. The pitch sloped quite considerably. With a lot of manhandling and some help from our very relieved French and Dutch neighbours, we raised Starboard to "almost level" on blocks and ramps by pivoting, while keeping the nearside ALKO wheel lock lined up and stationary with a wedge. Remarkably, this worked.

The difficulties associated with getting on some pitches are sometimes simply not obvious. Mark put it into context; "We had to avoid the car, the motorhome, the post and hedge while not grounding out. Other than that, it was a piece of cake." Mark chose now as the moment to tell me that there was a storm evacuation plan displayed in reception. I hoped that any storms would pass us by. Somehow, I couldn't see us getting out of there very quickly in an emergency!

I felt a bit frazzled by the time we had settled. When I went to get water for a much-needed cup of tea, a Danish couple whom we had met at reception were already pitched, awning up and enjoying a late afternoon snack in the sun!

Thankfully, the very English storm that had been brewing since Oléron had been averted. Mark had heroically offered to give up drinking tea to allow our dwindling supplies of tea bags to last me until we got home, thus saving me from the Ubiquitous Evil of Lipton's Yellow Label.

Friends had, however, recognised this for the true crisis it was and had rallied. At least a dozen had offered to post us out an emergency ration of PG Tips!

We had experienced a number of parallels with Mark's first trip to France at the age of 19. We had retraced some of his steps in Marsanne, during our Trip Down Memory Lane. He had come to France in a blue van, accompanied by a lady named Jackie (*whose name he failed to remember when he introduced us, despite our sharing the same name!*)

More worryingly, he chose to share with me now that

the clutch on his first blue van had also failed...! "Most of the bolts sheared off the gearbox as well!" he added jauntily.

Those were the days when a DIY car-fix was achievable – long before "Elf and Safety gone mad." You remember – The Good Old Days. When you shared the road with literally thousands of dangerous and poorly maintained vehicles!

Mark had clearly been on an even stricter budget in those days, so he had found his own DIY car-fix; "I connected the clutch and gearbox together with wire coat-hangers. Obviously, the two were not perfectly aligned... and the starter motor was held in by a bootlace. I drove all the way from Toulon to Calais in second gear. I had to get the dock workers to push the van on and off the ferry!"

Such a Heath Robinson approach was never going to be a permanent fix.

Mark's return from his dream trip had ended abruptly at Ashford in Kent, when the remaining bolts sheared. The gearbox had actually fallen out of the engine and on to the road.

I was still rather hoping that we could make it back to Verwood, Hampshire, where we had an appointment with a skilled mechanic, without resorting to anything like coat hangers or a bootlace!

As such - no touring; no sightseeing; no shopping. Big Blue was placed on immediate bed rest in the hope that her clutch would survive long enough to get us home!

26

MORE COCK-UPS ON THE CÔTE D'ÉMERAUDE

On the Maladroit Mastery of Multiple Moves; The Perilous Pitfalls of Polarity - & the Liabilities of Loss & Levelling!

Our campsite at St Coulomb was on a peninsula; we had a Left Beach and a Right Beach to choose from. We took our first evening stroll on Right Beach. It was unbelievably beautiful.

It was a golden autumn evening, with a deep blue sea rolling in and crashing on the sand. The jagged rocks of two small islands punctuated the bay, with white waves and spray swirling around them. Paragliders added colour to the skyline. For our Anniversary, there was even a lighthouse in the distance. (We were married in a lighthouse.)

We walked to both ends of the beach – the second end proving to have the most points of interest. We had, yet again, stumbled into a naturist area. On my 17th Wedding Anniversary, I had not expected to be confronted by another man's penis!

I described how it had already been a struggle to get on to our pitch here. But therein lies the danger of suddenly finding yourself at home to Mr Cock Up. Before you know it, he has moved in, eaten all your porridge and has first dibs on your bed... even before those pit-pinching puppies have got there!

We had some overnight rain. By Tuesday, we seemed to have developed a significant list to starboard. I had experienced a slight wobble while walking around the caravan on Sunday night. I commented to Mark that Kismet was like one of those fairground attractions with wonky rooms. Mark blamed the Anniversary Wine. However, when our coffees slid down the worktop this morning, I put forward to the Prosecution my case for having new and empirical evidence that it was definitely not the wine!

We had also fused the electrics three times. Luckily, being the end of the season, our neighbours had all moved, but we were now on the fourth – and final – electrical spur.

With Kismet leaning like the Tower of Pisa and a free pitch next door, with four brand new electrical spurs to fuse, we decided to move house. This would seem like a straightforward procedure. I took the doggies for a walk on a drizzly, deserted but beautiful Right Beach, while Mark disconnected everything and made ready to relocate. On my return, everything looked good. He was hitched and ready to roll.

An hour of manoeuvring later, our German neighbour had already been over twice to see if we were OK and whether we were finally in position. The answer, unfortunately, was "No!" We were going backwards and forwards like Austin Powers in the movie where he got his car stuck sideways on in a narrow corridor.

Then, levelling and lining up of the ALKO lock seemed to pose more of a problem than ever. We levelled the caravan and the ALKO was out of line. We lined up the

ALKO, then we weren't level. We lined everything up then the caravan fell off the levelling ramps. We lined everything up again and found that we had forgotten to remove the chocks, so poor Big Blue, who was supposed to be on bed rest with a poorly clutch, was pulling forward even harder than ever! The German couple, who had by now been out for the day, were incredulous when they came back and found our jump to the right was still some way to the left.

Anyway. After all that, we were still speaking to each other. Big Blue still had a clutch and we were so level that we could have been parked on a particularly level part of the Somerset Levels – after it had been carefully levelled by an obsessive leveller with a top-of-the-range levelling machine. I asked Mark if I could take a photo of him next to his handiwork but he declined, albeit politely. Perhaps after wine-o'clock. (We had both foolishly agreed to Stoptober this morning and were regretting it before the month had even started!)

On Wednesday, we did the most beautiful walk along the La Côte d'Émeraud – the Emerald Coast. The path from the campsite along the cliffs forms part of the emblematic GR34 (GR stands for Grande Randonnée – a series of French long-distance walking paths.) Mark asked me where the camera was and I told him that I hadn't brought it to stop him being grumpy about my constantly taking photos! It was a shame; the views were stupendous and we could really see the emerald colours in the sea that give this area its name.

In France, we have seen children having skiing lessons as part of the school curriculum. On Monday, the harbour at Left Beach was full of youngsters in sailing boats and kayaks. On Tuesday, kids were out beachcombing and today, they were on the beach doing races. I really like the French scholastic system.

We also saw the Pompiers (Firemen) on exercises. Their Fire Engines were in the car park, their boats on the beach – and they were all in the Beach Bar!

By Thursday, the weather was changing. It had started to feel much more autumnal, but it didn't matter to us. We had designated a day of jobs. The pups needed to go the vet for their mandatory tapeworm treatment, which is required to allow them to re-enter the UK.

The vet in St Malo was very unengaging. When we arrived, the receptionist said that we had no appointment and demanded to know if we'd come to the right practice. I showed her the number that we had called to make the appointment and confirmed the address; rue Tertre aux Nefles.

"I called on Monday and spoke to a lady who speaks good English." I knew she spoke good English because we had conducted the whole appointment-making process in my limping French. She had then brightly concluded the conversation with "See you at 3 o'clock on Thursday!"

They made us wait for an hour before charging €120 for four worming pills and the requisite stamps in the pet pass-ports. It wasn't just the dogs who had to swallow hard on that bitter pill!

Friday opened play with grey skies and a rainbow, but faired up again later. We decided to do the cliff walk again and I was allowed to take the camera this time! It was just as beautiful. I don't think that I could ever get tired of those views. The area was gorgeous - and with Big Blue on bed rest, we hadn't even explored it properly. A large cloud appeared, so we paced it out to get back to the caravan, since we had laundry out. Unlike next door, we had hung it between two trees out of our line of sight. They had set up their chairs and table looking out over the view – and then strung out their freshly washed pants right in front!

I had seen sparrows, robins and goldfinches hopping about. We had well and truly left cicada country. Still, the Breton drizzle was an excellent way to acclimatise ahead of our return to a British October!

A rather slick teardrop caravan from Holland arrived opposite. Also, unfortunately, with it being the weekend, our little area filled up. We worried that the congestion might make getting Kismet out again a bit of a picnic. I am pleased to report that there were many who did try to get on to our previous pitch, but literally *everyone* who attempted do so grounded out and gave up. We felt vindicated!

On Sunday morning, we decided to move the caravan to a third pitch to make the early departure for the ferry more straightforward the following day. Our new neighbours, Mike and June from Hayling Island, offered to help. Mike said that he would save our clutch by using his 4×4 to move Kismet. What a star! We just managed to squeeze out with a slight grounding of the back nearside corner of the caravan and an offside altercation with a hedge. I hoped that Caravan Kismet didn't mind having another man's flange ball in her hitch.

We had a cuppa with them and got on like a house on fire, an adage that turned out to be particularly apt for the four of us. It seemed that they too were somewhat prone to mishaps! Although aware of it, we have not encountered Reverse Polarity on our trip. I always check the electrics at each site, even though I didn't think polarity was anything much to worry about; just a precaution to stop you getting an electric shock from your kettle.

June and Mike soon disabused us of our complacence.

Their Carbon Monoxide (CO) alarm had gone off at 2am one night. Whatever they did, it wouldn't stop. They turned off the gas, checked everything that they could think of and eventually, disconnected the "malfunctioning" alarm.

A couple of days later, by sheer chance, they looked at their leisure battery and found that the casing was bowed, red hot and starting to melt. They had discovered the source of killer CO – and a potential source of ignition! They said that they always check polarity, but for some reason had just forgotten on that occasion. A cautionary tale!

They had also managed to book their return sailing a year late. Their suspicions had been aroused when they had spoken to someone on site who said that the ferry was at 10:30. They disagreed and said that their departure was at 08:30. Then they checked their ticket and found that their return trip was not until next October - a year hence!

Mark and keys are not compatible. As with every trip we have ever done, this one would not have been complete without a Magic Markie Moment involving keys. On our very last day, we had one which lasted for the whole evening. Due to depart first thing the following morning, Mark lost his keys. You know; the keys for the van / caravan / wheel lock / hitch lock.

We turned the caravan upside down twice before we went out for dinner with June and Mike. We were preoccupied throughout our whole bucket of moules, thinking that we'd return from the café to an empty pitch; caravan and all worldly possessions stolen. And we were now in Stoptober, so we couldn't even console ourselves with alcohol!

We strip- and cavity-searched the caravan twice more after dinner. I mean how many places are there to lose keys in a caravan? We had the mattress up, all the cushions off the sofas, went through the laundry several times and carefully scanned the route to the shower block... Then Mark opened the most incongruous cupboard of all. The small one above the fridge where we shove carrier bags – and I had a horrifying flash of recollection. I vacillated for a second. Was there any way that I could get away with it? I decided that there was nothing for it but to 'fess up.

The cupboard above the fridge was the safe place where I had hidden Mark's keys when we went to the beach that morning.

We discovered later that our caravan insurance is invalid if we leave the keys in the caravan – even if they are in a place so safe that we can't find them ourselves – so be warned!

27

BLIGHTED BACK IN BLIGHTY

The Course of Caravanning Never Did Run Smooth... but today,
Mr Cock Up did teach us a very valuable lesson!

We arrived back in Portsmouth at 18:30 on a golden October evening and were even the first off the ferry! Marvellous. All we had to do was drive for an hour or so to Verwood, get pitched and relax for the evening.

But the course of caravanning never did run smooth and tonight, we learnt a very important lesson;

WRITE DOWN THE NAME AND ADDRESS OF YOUR CAMPSITE!

I say this because if you simply rely on the campsite being programmed in the Sat Nav, you might find that the campsite is not, in fact, listed.

Then you might find that your husband can't remember whether he made the booking with the Caravan and Motorhome Club (CMC) or Camping and Caravanning Club (C&CC). Obviously, you can check both websites, but then you might find that there are three campsites in

Verwood and your husband can't remember the actual name of the site that he booked either.

He might claim that he has a confirmation email on his phone, but that is no good if you can't check it because there is no phone service. He might have written down the phone number of the campsite and the booking reference (but not the name) in his diary, but without phone service, that is also no help.

You might stop a few times and find that you have phone coverage, but then discover that when you do get through, it is just an Ansa phone.

Then you might find that his phone battery dies. Knowing your husband's stance on Social Media and photography, you might not want to mention that your phone is already dead from trying to take a picture of Portsmouth's Spinnaker Tower to put on Facebook, so that service or no, YOU can't check emails or make any calls either!

One option is just to go blindly to your destination town (Verwood) and drive aimlessly around narrow country lanes in the dark, towing a 7.3m caravan with a 5m van, hoping to find the correct campsite by accident.

By now, if you have an in-car charger, your husband might have managed to charge up his phone sufficiently to find an email from a caravan site in his inbox. You might look at it and say "It is just a publicity email and the phone number isn't the same as the one written in the diary" but your husband might disagree and say "Why would we have an email from a campsite if it were not a confirmation? And they sign off from the list of all the attractions in the local area by saying that they are looking forward to welcoming us."

So to keep the peace, you might give in and agree go

there and find that a lady comes out and asks you what on earth you are doing hauling a large caravan up her drive in the middle of the night. You might look hopeful and say something along the lines of "I think we have a reservation here tonight..." and she might look in the van and see your four beloved pets and reply "You definitely don't. We don't take dogs!"

But then, there are good Samaritans in the world and she might call upon her husband and his mobile phone - all the while complaining about the terrible phone service around Verwood - and find a campsite with a phone number that matches the one in your diary and give you directions that you can't remember to get there. Then, by a stroke of luck and a few arguments about which round-abouts you had to turn right and which you had to turn left, you might find yourself at the "Verwood Camping and Cara-vanning Club Site" and have immediate sympathy with your husband's inability to recall either the name of such a campsite in Verwood or whether it was run by the CMC or C&CC!

And the lovely, lovely wardens might open the gate for you even though you were supposed to arrive before 8pm and it is now nearly 9 and lead you on to a nice flat pitch where you don't need to level the caravan.

Then, all you have to do is pitch the caravan in the dark, walk four hyperactive dogs, who have been on the ferry or in the van all day – and really wish that you hadn't given up alcohol.

28

HOME – AND BRIEFLY BACK "IN THE BRICK"

Pecuniary Pandemonium; The Subconscious Rejection of a Conventional Lifestyle & STOPtober

We arrived home to a harsh dose of reality. Having no income, we do our best to save the odd Euro here and there, but we came back to a Holy Trinity of pecuniary pandemonium;

1. A speeding fine from a minor transgression which happened just before we left, three months ago; now transmuted into a Court Summons because, being abroad, we had neither received nor responded to it;
2. A fine for deducting our tax allowance from our tax return, when we should have left THAT to HMRC and;
3. A fine for our vehicle tax running out. To be truthful, we had been naïve enough to think that we didn't need to renew our UK tax while the van was out of the country...

We felt like Bonnie and Clyde – mindful that notorious criminal Al Capone was ultimately brought to justice on a charge of tax evasion.

Still, Mark cut his own hair with the dog scissors. That was £15 saved!

4th October – If we had anything controversial to do, today was the day to do it. It seemed that all our luck had been thrown into a basket; all the bad luck had come out over the last couple of weeks and all the good luck had come out this morning.

We stepped out of the caravan to find that the hole for the ALKO wheel lock had come to rest lined up perfectly. Then Mark took Big Blue to the van doctor; the diagnosis – she was WELL. Her clutch was worn, but didn't need to be replaced. She had just been working very hard. We were told "The clutch should last 100,000 miles but might have a slightly shortened life because of towing and carrying weight." I was delighted. After all the fines, I hadn't been looking forward to the number of noughts that I thought we would find on the end of that particular bill!

I went shopping and attracted more than a few funny looks. Not least because it was a cool autumn day – I had seen my own breath this morning – yet I was dressed in shorts and flip flops. Having been in 35°C heat until recently, I had not yet found my cool weather gear. The looks may also have been something to do with the cream colour of my outfit, which sported quite a number of black paw prints from darling little Lani, who had seen fit to trample her muddy paws all over me in the van.

The cost of produce in France had been exorbitant. Even in areas where they were grown locally, a melon cost double the price that you would expect to pay in the UK and unlike in Britain, we found the French markets to be more expensive than supermarkets. I actually enjoyed doing a shop in Sainsbury's and getting a basket full of lovely, fresh fruit that didn't cost an arm and a leg. Plus Dorset Cereal (which isn't insanely sweet muesli full of choc chips) and Melton Mowbray pies!

I don't really like Melton Mowbray pies but experienced a sudden, inexplicable craving for them when we were in the Drôme. Luckily we discovered Pâté en Croute, which was similar enough to sate the craving. However there is nothing like the real thing. I also bought a whole chicken for WAY less than €17 and two fine pieces of Sirloin. Hurrah! Meat, meat, meat, meat. At French prices, our budget had afforded us only a few lardons and occasional charcuterie. At last. MEAT!

I also bought some Tetley Tea, which was going to prove very costly. Mark asked me "What did you get that for?" I replied that I had managed to procure some in France when we ran out of tea and we had been quite enjoying it. He ridiculed me and said that we hadn't had Tetley Tea at any time that he could remember. I bet him £1m that it was Tetley's and told him that I had a photo of it as proof. Unfortunately, on producing a photo of a packet of PG Tips, my gambling debts regarding the lead actor in The Silence of the Lambs, the wager about the height of Munros in Unlucky Al-levard and some other absolute certainty of mine that I can't remember now amounted to £4m.

I rang my Dad and he asked me if I had remembered to say 'rabbit' on the first of the month. I said that I had forgotten. Maybe this was the reason for our recent run of bad luck and my now massive gambling debt!

Our homecoming was followed by two weeks of hectic

socialising, appointments and trips around the country, catching up with friends and family. We even had to get up before 8am for several days on the trot. It was an outrage!

We made our now annual pilgrimage to the Motorhome and Caravan Show at the NEC and, even after living with Kismet full-time for five months, agreed that she would still be our caravan of choice.

Then, it was time to move "Back in the Brick" to add a little class to our abode and make it ready for the next tenant.

Moving house is always stressful, but this time the stress was of our own making.

Is it eccentric to sit in your caravan on the drive, drinking cups of tea? The Estate Agent had forgotten to tell us that the tenant checkout had already been completed the day before, so we were actually free to enter our own home at will!

Then, we had been "Back in the Brick" for less than an hour and I managed to lock us out and the dogs in. And I had always claimed that Mark was irresponsible with keys.

Really, I think it reflected a subconscious rejection of a conventional lifestyle...

There are not many things in life that I regret, but when dear friends have driven for ninety minutes to come and welcome you home, then not only can you not invite them in for a coffee (because you have locked yourself out) but you can't spend time with them before they leave as you have to shoot off immediately to get a spare set of keys from the Estate Agent to free your incarcerated puppies...

One thing that I was going to do now that we were 'Back in the Brick' was to partake of the only thing that I had missed while living full-time in a caravan... I vowed to have a bath EVERY SINGLE DAY!

17th **October** – We had made it seventeen days into Stop-tober (plus a couple of days extra in Stoptember) until Rosie led us astray.

With what was about to come our way, it was probably for the best.

29

ADVENTURES OFF GRID – SETTHORNS, NEW FOREST

"I am not the same having seen the moon shine on the other side of the world." Mary Anne Radmacher Hershey

Well, we arrived last Friday.

The Answer: "Wednesday!"

11th **November** – We were back in the caravan. We camped at the beautiful Setthorns in the midst of the New Forest and had decided to go off-grid. This would save us around 50% on site fees. We had purchased a Safefill refillable gas bottle and opted for a simple life; our energy needs would now be met solely by gas, a leisure battery and a solar panel.

The Question: we asked on Friday was – "We wonder how long the battery will last..!"

By Wednesday evening, the caravan was completely dead. We were crawling around in freezing temperatures, warmed only by dogs and the gas hob with illumination provided by a torch. Our schoolboy error had been to leave the 24-hour thermostat active on the heating. Although the heating runs from gas, the pump, it would appear, uses rather a lot of electricity, especially in the chill hours of darkness. You know, when your solar panel can't recharge the battery.

Although we did save some fuel by switching off everything and going away to visit a friend for one night, we had unfortunately forgotten that the fridge needed gas and so, not for the first time, me pancetta and peas defrosted.

So we spent all the money that we had saved on electricity in the pub, which wasn't the worst possible outcome! We treated ourselves to heat and light plus a steak and heart pudding with chips at The Three Tuns in Bransgore, one of my favourite pubs in the world. I think we made an odd couple, sitting on the sofas in the snug, festooned with dogs. Mark availed himself of the much-missed internet and I wrote my Christmas cards early – the aim being to inform everyone not to send us a card, since we were once again of no fixed abode.

Earlier that day, I had tried on a T-Shirt in a shop and noticed in the mirror that my trousers had mud spattered up the back and were covered in muddy paw prints. I apologised to the assistant; "It looks like a designer pattern!" she quipped generously...

Nevertheless, I was beginning to feel that I was no longer fit to be unleashed on polite society!

Like Mary Ann Radmacher Hershey "I am not the same having seen the moon shine on the other side of the world."

I know that it was just France this time, but I used to feel similarly out of place when I returned from life-changing experiences in wonderful, exotic places like Nepal, South America and Africa – and was then forced to slot straight back into the humdrum life of work : eat : sleep : repeat.

Thursday – We went to get the van MOT'd and have her shocks replaced. It was delightful to be caught out by a really heavy shower as we walked the dogs back from the beach to the garage. My trousers were so wet that I had waterfalls cascading into my boots! Thankfully, Big Blue was ready sooner than we had expected, which gave us the chance to move the caravan to an electric pitch. It was such a pleasant experience, relocating the caravan in cold, wet trousers. At least we hadn't been subjected to the tornadoes which had swept across the Midlands and Wales.

It was such a treat to have heat and light restored. I would like to proffer a suggestion that in hindsight, it was rather ill-advised to attempt to go off-grid in a dim forest during the short days of a UK November. (Like a 3* kayak course that we booked in Wales one February and nearly got hypothermia. What POSSESSED US?) Off-grid is something that we might try again next year, perhaps in the long, balmy days and sizzling sun of a hot, European summer.

My other Top Tip of the Day is that silica gel kitty litter in a pop sock stuffed into your soaking wet boots dries them out a treat overnight!

The Three L's - Leicestershire; Lincolnshire; Lancashire

Our progression continued North up to Leicestershire. It was FREEZING and went dark a lot earlier than in the South. Mark got everything set up really quickly – then found that he hadn't fitted the ALKO wheel lock. While he sorted it out, I walked the dogs, wearing my woolly hat and buff against the searing, cold wind. When I came back, the farmer was wandering around in a T-Shirt. They breed 'em tough "Up North". I have become soft. A Northerner by birth, clearly, I have dwelt in the Softie Shandy-Drinking South for too long!

Saturday – There was frost on the ground when Mark walked the dogs – in his shorts. It was a momentous day.

Our Endless Summer was now officially over. Mark had finally conceded to make the move into long trousers.

The purpose of our visit to Leicestershire was to visit Inner Wolf, a top, doggy sports shop to try on snow coats for the dogs in preparation for our ski trip in January. There were no padded jackets, but we plumped for slush suits, which seem to do the trick. They certainly came in very useful when walking the dogs in the soggy fields around Wistow church. Unfortunately, Lani's slush suit was on back order, so she got full contact when she made up her mind to roll in a dead rat.

We decided that boots were expensive and probably unnecessary, but I really wish that I had taken a video of Lani trying out a set – she was high-stepping around the shop like a mini dressage horse!

We smiled and laughed, oblivious to the fact that our shopping trip around Leicestershire, Lincolnshire and Lancashire would soon turn into what we later dubbed "Black Monday."

30

BLACK MONDAY – TROUBLE AT
T'MILL, LANCASHIRE

"Travel Broadens the Vocabulary." Jackie Lambert

A woman once said this. That woman was me. And I said it today – the most vocabulary-broadening day of our trip so far.

Only yesterday, we had met up with friends in Castle Donington and had been telling them what a wonderful lifestyle ours is; touring in a caravan; seeing new and wonderful places; enjoying the freedom of the open road.

This morning, we woke up in a waterlogged field in Leicestershire with Storm Angus raging around us on what shall be known forthwith in the annals of Lambertshire as "Black Monday".

I wasn't sure that we would even be able to get off the soggy, grass pitch in our field in Leicestershire. We did, but it was the only thing that went well all day.

And so, I shall regale you with the tale of what we got up to on our Three Counties Tour – and what happens when Livin' the Dream turns into a nightmare!

Our purpose had been a shopping trip around all the L's.

Leicestershire (doggie snow suits), Lincolnshire (wheels & winter tyres for Big Blue) and Lancashire for an Amazon "Click and Collect" in a Post Office – since, being of no fixed abode, we have no delivery address. (We thought we'd also visit my Dad. He does live quite close to said Post Office!)

The Sat Nav had been locking intermittently for some time, although it had now finally broken completely. This made finding our field somewhere in the wilds of Leicestershire tricky after visiting our friends in Donington. Nevertheless, a quick check of AA Route Finder on the computer assured us that our next destination, Gainsborough, was fewer than two hours away from our Leicestershire campsite. Three hours later, we were still en route, trying to text our eBay seller of van wheels and winter tyres to find out where he was – and make sure that he would be in when we called. We got no reply.

We drove through Laughterton, which is always joyful. It is where our lives changed for ever when we picked up our beautiful boy, Kai a year and a half ago. We eventually received a text from Mr eBay and continued to the back end of Gainsborough in the pouring rain, with our 7.3m caravan in tow. We finally found our man, who furnished us with four winter wheels for our impending Alpine adventure. Luckily, there was just enough room for us to execute a U-Turn with our 40ft rig in Duck (rhymes with...well, let's say LUCK!) Lane.

All we had to do then was drive over the Pennines to Lancashire on the M62. In my opinion, the M62 is the most dangerous motorway in the country - and we had to cross it in the teeth of a storm! We had long abandoned any hope of getting to our next campsite in time to set up while it was still light. I managed to find a Sat Nav app on Mark's phone. It worked quite well until the battery died in the snow on top of the notorious Saddleworth Moor. Here, we sat for an hour in traffic due to an accident.

In the dark, with driving rain, surface water and strong winds buffeting the caravan, I was, in a way, relieved. It forced the traffic to slow down. As usual on the M62, people were not driving to the conditions and as we approached the accident, we saw the consequences. No fewer than twelve fire engines were trying to recover a number of vehicles which had nose-dived straight off the motorway and plummeted down the steep sides of the moor. We crawled on past Manchester and north to Preston at 30mph. We found our campsite – after seven hours solid in the van. It was a relief.

Or so we thought!

"It is all hard standing, although the grass has grown through the hard standing a bit" were our pitching instructions. "Just choose your spot." We drove round the campsite, barely able to see and picked our spot.

On Noirmoutier, we had helped to dig a young German couple's camper van out of the sand. Congratulating ourselves on what experienced caravanners we now were, we had chortled "We'd never get stuck!" We were far too savvy for that.

So as we reversed on to our pitch and pulled forward slightly to re-position, Big Blue immediately got bogged down in thick mud!

We stood outside in the dark, in torrential rain, surveying the situation; "If we unhitch, we might be able to drive Big Blue off..." But we couldn't unhitch because reversing had compressed the tow hitch. A caravanning phenomenon that we had discovered way back on our Maiden Voyage!

After a good deal of faffing in the pitch darkness and driving rain, we did finally manage to separate the van from the caravan, but there was no moving anything. Big Blue was well and truly stuck. We tried to push the caravan, but that was always a bit of a tall order – 1.5 tonnes on wet grass? No way! We managed to spin her around. At least she was level and our cable could reach the electricity, although the caravan door had come to rest next to a rather large and muddy puddle. Ah well, at least we were sorted.

Or so we thought.

I stepped into the caravan and wondered why my slippers were wet. The answer was quite straightforward. The caravan was flooded! We had just replaced the two front carpets, which had become a little worn. Our brand-new carpets were sodden with black, gritty water – it looked like water that had come in from the road. We tried to find the source of the leak and in the meantime found that all our documents in the offside locker were soaked and the camera and electronics in the front locker were almost floating.

We rolled up our lovely new carpets and put them in the shower cubicle then mopped the floor, which used up all our clean towels. We didn't have any food, but we had half a bottle of wine. At least we could sit and relax.

Or so we thought.

As I went to get the wine glasses, I noticed a foreign object on the bed. With all that had been going on, we had not given the dogs the consideration that they deserved. Today could only be described as Scheisse – and one of the pups, who had all been as good as gold all day, had been forced, in desperation, to underline it.

They say that it will all look better in the morning. I suppose that at least the rain had stopped, but sixteen paws and four feet still had to enter and exit the caravan via the muddy puddle. All of the local dog walks involved thick mud and Big Blue was still immovable. The short route back on to the hard standing behind Big Blue was blocked by the caravan. The only route available to effect the release of Big Blue was the long way, across an expanse of sodden grass.

Mark went out just after breakfast and by 12.30, was still trying to dig the van out.

Improvisation is the key to caravanning. With Big Blue stuck, we had no vehicle. The site was deserted and we knew of no-one on whom we could call to rock up with a handy, emergency Land Rover to tow us off. Like the Apollo 13 Mission, we had to solve our dilemma using only the items that we had to hand.

You may mock, but I hope that this might go some way to explain the litany of rather peculiar methods that we enlisted in our attempts to escape! We unloaded Big Blue to reduce her weight before deploying an esoteric series of items to try to prevent her from sinking into the mud. This included a hard-backed A5 note pad, bits of memory foam mattress and my bath mat. Against my advice, Mark employed a pole from the awning as a digging implement – so that got a nice kink in it as well.

I ordered some gripper tracks locally, but we had no way of getting them. My Dad has passed his four score, so I couldn't ask him to drive to a Caravan dealership on a remote industrial estate and then try to find us in the middle of a field, down a muddy lane.

As we were digging, the lady owner came down and asked us the most ridiculous question in the world:

"What did you go on there for?!"

We didn't say it, but the answer on the tip of our tongues was "Because we wanted to spend seven hours digging our van out of mud instead of seeing Jackie's Dad, which was the reason that we drove three hundred miles North!"

On further reflection, she did seem to accept that if

guests arrive on a filthy, stormy night, in the dark with rain coming in horizontally, distinguishing "hard standing with grass growing through it" from "grass" may not be a given!

She conceded that "I should really mark out the pitches a bit better." I would say just marking them out at all would have been a big help. At least she provided us with a shovel.

Chocks away. We had found a chock in the field in Leicestershire, but we were now down on the deal. We had since lost two, which had been engulfed by Lancashire mud.

By mid-afternoon, we were out of the mud. Then, all we had to do was make good our mess and go and collect our gripper tracks. The irony was that gripper tracks weigh nothing and cost only £9.99. The caravan shop advised us; "Yes – it's always worth keeping some with you..."

Well now we know.

And the other lesson that we have learned is that we really are not too bright to get ourselves stuck!

After all these miry misfortunes, our clothes and pretty much every fabric item in the caravan was covered with either mud or gritty water from mopping up the flood. I managed to see Dad for half an hour, in between keeping five washes on the go simultaneously at the launderette. I was conscious of a sign in the launderette that specified "No Pet Bedding or Horse Blankets" – nothing about bath mats that had been ground into Lancashire clay beneath a van wheel. I managed to load the machines when no-one was looking, which was a good job. During the wash cycle, the front-loaders looked like they had been filled with Turkish coffee.

Thankfully, the Proprietress of the Launderette didn't appear until the second rinse, when the water had achieved a more acceptable hue. She had a solid, square, middle-aged torso attired in a sleeveless, pale blue nylon overall. This showed off crêpey, white arms, festooned with intimidating, indigo tattoos. Beneath cropped, bleached-blonde hair were pale eyes, which darted like meteors around the launderette. They zeroed in quick succession on the rim of mud around my boots; connecting that with a few piles of earth on the floor and a twig and stray leaf shed from my bemired bits and pieces. Her eyes bored into me for a second but luckily, she decided not to strike. I really didn't fancy messing with her. Somehow, I knew instinctively not to volunteer a compliment that her washing machine had brought up my muddy bath mat like new!

The morning did finally arrive when everything looked better; all the mud had frozen, we had moved the caravan away from the puddle – and we were LEAVING!

We had dinner with Dad in one of my favourite Lancashire pubs; The Royal Oak in Riley Green. Curry, a fry up, a roast dinner and The Royal Oak's mouth-watering Steak Pudding are the four Great British foods that we had dreamed about in France. We washed it down with a foaming pint of Thwaite's "Wainwright" bitter, named for Blackburn's famous son, Alfred Wainwright.

As I told you back in Loudun, Wainwright is the author of the beautiful, hand-drawn mountain guide-books to the Lake District and Scotland – and it was he who put our tribulations into perspective. Our beer glass bore a quote from the great man;

"You were made to soar, to crash to earth, then to rise and soar again."

Research has proven that swearing has many benefits *(there was an article on this in Time Magazine, no less!)* and c'mon, when learning a foreign language, you always learn the naughty words first. Personally, I can swear effectively in French, Welsh, German and Italian as well as

English, so I remained sanguine about our sudden crash to earth.

As I said, travel broadens the vocabulary – and with the ability to lower my blood pressure and increase my pain threshold in five languages, soar I shall!

31

AND IN CONCLUSION...

Brrrrr! We had frost on our awning today, but we were cuddly-cosy in the caravan. It was the coldest November day for six years, apparently.

We were reflective as our first year of unexpected adventures drew to a close and we made ready for Christmas at Hunter's Moon CMC Site, Wareham.

And in conclusion – it is really difficult to write a conclusion!

We thought that we had lost everything when our working lives ended unexpectedly, leaving us jobless and too ill to work, but as that chapter closed, we realised that adventure starts at the end of your comfort zone.

After more than thirty years of targets and deadlines, we were getting better at not feeling guilty about getting up late, relaxing and doing as we pleased. One thing that we simply could not drop from that ingrained working mind-set, however, is that when we finish one trip, we need to have the next trip planned and sorted, so that we continually have something to look forward to.

It is – and always has been – The Law!

Mark told me that he had booked "The wol-SER-tl" for the winter. It was a few days and much interrogation later that I realised that this was somewhere that we had stayed before – twice!

"You mean the VALSER-tal?" I asked. "Yes" he replied. "That's what I said."

It was The French Batmobiles (battlefields) and The Bed Shovels (vegetables) all over again.

You would think that having spent four months in a caravan together, our communication skills might have been better. Perhaps that is why Ernest Hemingway said "Never go on trips with anyone you do not love." Certainly we had weathered the breakages, near death experiences and extreme British weather without so much as a cross word. We had also accepted that we are not sufficiently smart to avoid getting stuck in the mud and that neither of us is sensible enough to take charge of keys.

So now that our trip to the Italian Alps for the winter was certain, we had been planning; we had stocked up on winter doggie clothing, researched doggie booties, paw wax and tried to buy wheels and winter tyres for our van, Big Blue. Although we had picked them up in a storm, the wheels from Gainsborough were a lot more straightforward than the winter tyres, which were delivered, eventually, from Berlin (after three orders sent to two different companies – who turned out to be one and the same company!)

They say that you can't make an omelette without breaking eggs and it would seem that you can't make a caravanner without breaking quite a lot of other things – and that includes the rules.

Our new lifestyle is unconventional, but we love it and

are not sure that we will be changing it any time soon. We travel not to escape life, but so that life does not escape us and, although we haven't been everywhere yet, it is most definitely on our list!

32

SO, WHAT DID WE LEARN?

We Made the Mistakes so that You Don't Have To!

We had never owned a caravan before. However, in this book you have seen how we gave up work, accidentally bought a caravan and made the decision to live in it and tour Europe

Going from First Timers to Full-Timers in a month was a steep learning curve, however, here I will share some of the lessons that we learned in our first year.

1. Travelling with dogs is an absolutely WONDERFUL way to meet people! We now have new friends – and invitations to visit – all over the world.
2. If you caravan at altitude, your toilet will explode, so remember to leave the cassette blade slightly open – or open it very tentatively.
3. Behind my husband, the dogs and the caravan, a caravan-specific Sat Nav is the last thing that I would part with.

4. We tried expensive spirit levels and found that they read differently, depending on orientation. We tried levelling apps that told us we were level when the caravan looked like an rocket on the launch pad. A tennis ball rolled down the centre of the caravan worked quite well as did the bullseye spirit level that we got free at the Motorhome & Caravan Show… but the most civilised way to check that you are level is to place a glass of wine on the worktop. You can't read that in a book. Cheers!

5. Carry a pair of gripper tracks. You are never too clever to get stuck. You might think that you are. But you're not!

6. They have dogs in France, so dog food is widely available to purchase. So you DO NOT need to take 100kg of dry dog food with you.

7. HOWEVER; you DO need to take 100kg of proper English tea with you… So don't blame me if you run out and get stuck drinking Lipton's Yellow Label!

8. If you can't get dog food (or pretty much *anything else* for that matter – like a battery for your laptop or your favourite pair of sandals – although not PG Tips…) you can order it on the internet and have it delivered to the Campsite Reception or a "drop off location" such as a Post Office. You can even order in Sterling on Amazon UK and, if you set the delivery address as your primary address, Amazon will tell you which merchants deliver to the country that you are in.

9. Melamine is the Work of the Devil. We found that Wedgewood china is perfect for

caravanning. It is particularly perfect if every other piece of crockery that you own broke when your husband dropped it out of the back of the van just before your trip.

10. A Bridgedale Merino Hiker makes a perfect cover for the safe transport of crystal glasses. Well you don't want to be drinking all those lovely French and Italian wines out of plastic, now, do you? (*Alternative, woolly walking socks are available.*)

11. Even if your phone company tell you that you CAN tether your laptop to your phone to get internet access abroad (in answer to your specific question about whether tethering abroad is possible) – you probably can't. So don't believe them. This will save you from paying for 20GB of data per month, which you can't use, on a contract from which they won't release you because you signed it, you idiot!

12. Silica gel kitty litter is CHEAP and GREAT for drying things out (we buy ours from Home Bargains.) Put some in a pop sock; it will keep cupboards and lockers dry, it will dry and de-odourise boots, trainers and ski gloves. We pile some in open plastic food containers to keep caravan Kismet condensation- and mould-free during winter storage.

13. **"Luck happens when Planning meets Opportunity."** Unlucky 13? We have proved that Livin' the Dream need not be impossible. *It is within your grasp,* provided that you are realistic, plan how to get there – and are willing to make some sacrifices!

33

TEN TIPS TO SAVE MONEY WHILE CARAVANNING

We are wiser today than we were yesterday...

We bought our caravan by accident and had only a month to sort everything out. As complete newbies, our first year was a little hit-and-miss and we *paid far too much* for nearly everything!

However, we are both thrifty and quick learners. Here, I will share with you some money-saving tips that in our second year reduced our outgoings by several thousands of pounds!

1. Caravan Storage

a. **Annual Storage** – our insurance initially insisted on our having CASSOA Gold secure storage sorted before we took delivery of the caravan. We arranged this in a hurry with a storage facility some distance from home, since this was the only one that we could find which had a vacancy at the time. This cost over £500 for the year, yet the caravan was in storage for only a few months!

b. **Monthly Storage** – we found a storage facility close to home that charged monthly, so we didn't have to travel miles and paid only for what we used. It did not have CASSOA Gold level of security, but we inspected it ourselves and were satisfied that our Pride and Joy was safe there. We pay a little more for our insurance, but the net saving is around £300pa.

c. **Storage at Home** – a few friends with space have kindly offered to store our caravan for us. Initially, this proved tricky with our insurers although we have now sorted this out and have saved 100% on our storage fees. Storage at your own home, if you live there, is not usually a problem with insurers.

d. **Storage Abroad** - to save on regular cross-channel transport is also a stumbling block with our insurers, however, it is something that we have been looking into, so watch this space!

2. Safefill Refillable Gas Bottle

a. This has saved us several hundreds of pounds on gas and enabled further saving by going off grid. Prices vary but refilling with 10kg (19.5L) of LPG at a petrol station costs us in the region of €8. Last time we bought a 6kg Calor bottle, it cost about £30 + deposit – and Calor is not available in Europe.

b. The Safefill cylinder is also significantly lighter than a Calor cylinder – and since you can refill it, you don't need a spare. The transparent bottle allows you to see how full it is.

c. You do need to buy a set of adapters for Europe with your cylinder.

d. We bought our cylinder from our dealer, who kindly

gave us 10% discount and modified our gas locker to accommodate the Safefill cylinder.

3. Going Off-Grid

a. In summer, in Europe, we have found that we rarely need electric hook-up (EHU). This saves a couple of Euros per night, which adds up to a few hundred pounds a year when you are away for months at a time.

b. Our energy costs were much reduced by the Safefill refillable gas bottle detailed above.

c. We simply get EHU for a single night if we need to use the hoover or do laundry.

d. We bought a power invertor which converts the 12V output of the leisure battery to 240V to charge up our laptops, but this has to be used with caution, as it drains the battery very quickly.

4. Washing Machine

a. We were spending around £20 per week on laundry. We bought a Costway portable twin-tub washing machine for around £100, so it paid for itself in just over a month! The machine weighs about 16kg and the drum and spin dryer are just large enough to take a polycotton Superkingsize duvet cover. It drains by gravity; we saw no need for the extra weight of a drain pump, which is just something else to go wrong. The washing machine has received many a look of envy from seasonal residents in Penthièvre. Another thing that I like about it is that Mark enjoys using it, so I need never do laundry again!

· · ·

5. Avoid Touristy Areas in High Season

a. We prefer to avoid the crowds anyway, but site fees in tourist hotspots can be double in high season. Also, the charge for dogs is often waived in low season – and this can be as much as €4 per dog per night.

b. ACSI – We also joined ACSI; "Europe's leading camp-site specialist". Besides listing nearly 10,000 sites across Europe, all of which are inspected annually, the ACSI card offers discounts in low season.

6. Avoid Toll Roads – and Traffic Fines!

a. **Tolls** – If you are not in a rush to get anywhere, you can get more of a feel for a country by driving at your leisure through the REAL countryside and all the quaint little towns. I certainly prefer that to speeding past everything on a motorway. We have a Caravan Specific Sat Nav which generally keeps us out of trouble. Tolls very quickly add up, particularly with a large vehicle such as a caravan or motorhome, which are charged at a higher rate.

b. **Vignette** – Be wary of those countries where you have to purchase a vignette before you use the roads – there are heavy fines if you fail to display the vignette and foreign vehicles are an easy target to pick out. Vignettes can usually be purchased at or close to the border. Read the instructions and make sure that you fill in the vignette if required and display it in the correct position on your windscreen. Sometimes, there are tolls on some roads in addition to the vignette.

c. **Bridge, Ferry and Tunnel charges** - These can also add up, so make sure that you include them in your travel calculations – particularly if you plan to cross bridges in Scandinavia! Do your research – we bought a 10-transit caravan pass for the Mont Blanc tunnel. It is valid for 2-years and if you are doing more than 1 transit (even without the caravan) you will save. It is not vehicle-specific, so we delighted some friends who were going skiing by donating a return trip that we were not going to use. Avoiding peak times on Ferries or the Channel Tunnel can result in very significant savings and if you are a regular ferry traveller, it may be worthwhile joining something like Brittany Ferries' Club Voyage, which gives discounts of up to 30%.

d. **Congestion Charges & Urban Road Tolls** – As in London, these have been introduced in certain cities and areas around Europe to improve congestion, air quality and reduce noise. In 2017, France introduced Crit'Air clean air stickers in some cities with fines of over €100 if you fail to display one. They can be ordered online, however order only from the Crit'Air website and allow at least 6 weeks for delivery.

e. **Abide by the Rules of the Road to Avoid Fines** –The A.A (Automobile Association) gives comprehensive country-by-country advice on tolls, driving, Rules of the Road and items that you are obliged by law to carry in your car for more than 40 countries, from Andorra to Ukraine. These guides will certainly help you to avoid further potential road-traffic fines.

7. Seasonal Pitches & Economical Places to Stay

a. **Seasonal Pitches** – When we came back from Europe after our first year's travelling, we stayed for a couple of months on a site, paying the usual fee of around £20 per night. Then someone mentioned "Seasonal Pitch". This was new to us, so we looked into it and the following year, we booked one. The Seasonal Pitch was overlooking last year's pitch, but it saved us nearly 50% on our UK site fees for 3-months; a £1000 saving – with hard-standing and EHU included! The UK Campsite website lists sites which offer seasonal pitches. Members of C&CC and CMC can benefit from storage and seasonal pitches at Club sites – although you do need to book early.

b. **Economical Campsites**

- **Certified Locations (CLs)** – are informal, privately owned UK caravan sites for up to five caravans. 2,500 of these are listed by the Caravan and Motorhome Club.
- **The Friendly Open All Year Under £15 Sites** - is a Facebook group which does what it says on the tin! A web search may also yield results for similar, inexpensive sites in the UK.
- **Municipal Campsites in France** – these council-run sites usually offer good facilities and excellent value. There are Municipal sites in most towns and larger villages throughout France. www.campingfrance.com/UK and www.camping-municipal.org list most of the Municipal sites.

c. **Cheaper Countries** – the relative strength of the pound and the comparative economies of some European countries means that we Brits find some places cheap and some places expensive! My advice would be to think carefully if you want to visit Scandinavia, Switzerland or most Capital Cities on a budget.

8. Internet – MiFi Unit

a. **Tethering a Mobile Phone** – as I stated in 'What Did We Learn' our mobile phone company would not allow us to tether our laptop to the phone to get internet access abroad. Check before you go, since it might save you from paying for 20GB of data per month, which you can't use, on a contract from which they won't release you! This meant that we were stuck without internet for the whole of our first year touring. However, we came up with a number of solutions.

b. **Free Internet on Campsites & Elsewhere** – Free Wi-Fi on campsites is generally so feeble that it is not worth having. As an alternative, we found reasonable free Wi-Fi in most Tourist Information Centres, McDonald's Restaurants and some hotels if you buy a drink. However, be aware that these free networks are usually 'open', so are not necessarily secure. If you use 'open' networks, change your passwords frequently and avoid doing sensitive things like internet banking.

c. **Paid Internet on Campsites** – in our first year, we paid for internet occasionally, if the charges were reasonable. Charges varied widely, but we found that €5 or €10 here and there for a few GB of data or 24-hours of internet access soon mounted up.

d. **MiFi Mobile Internet**

- For our second year of touring, we purchased an *unlocked MiFi unit*. Since it is 'unlocked', it can be used on any network and with any data SIM card to give you secure internet access.
- Our UK data SIM which we bought on a contract gave us 12GB of data in Europe (20GB in the UK) each month for £16. You need to check whether there is a limit on how many months a UK SIM

card will work abroad before having to be repatriated. Ours was good for four months, so it covered the duration of our trip. We did find, however, that we were frequently subjected to punishing extra charges for going over our data limit; even when we put a cap on it!

- We discovered that the best value internet is often achieved by purchasing a pay-as-you-go data SIM card for the country that you're in. €15 per month bought us 30GB in Italy but the best bargain was Romania, where €15 per month gave us 150GB of data. We have heard that internet is expensive in Germany, but have never bought a SIM there, so we can't give first hand advice.

- As with a mobile phone, Wi-Fi signals are generally good but not ubiquitous. Coverage is notoriously poor in East Germany – but AMAZING in Romania!

9. Use a Prepaid Money Card

a. Using your UK Credit Card abroad will attract both a fixed usage fee and a currency-exchange commission charge on every transaction. We carry a Sainsbury's 'Multi Currency Cash Passport' which is a secure, prepaid cash card. The exchange rates are competitive and it can be topped up in any currency you wish online, using Sterling from your UK Bank Account. You use it like any other chip and pin card to pay for goods or to withdraw cash from ATMs. Other similar pre-paid cards are available. The Money Supermarket website is a good resource for further advice and 'best buys' on prepaid cards.

. . .

10. Internet Shopping

a. You may be surprised to learn that you can order on the internet at keen prices and, if you ask nicely, have deliveries made to campsite reception (or drop off locations) all over Europe.

b. We now buy all our premium dog food on line (often from local companies) at a fraction of the cost of the equivalent in the shops.

c. When my favourite sandals broke, I had a brand new pair, exactly the same, delivered within two days to a post office in Hohnstein, East Germany. Amazon UK will even tell you which suppliers will deliver to the country that you're in – just register the delivery address as your primary address.

d. Extra delivery charges may apply, but the overall savings and convenience will usually leave you quids in.

e. Please note that ordering on the internet worked well in France, Germany and Italy, but we did experience some difficulty in getting deliveries made to the less 'mainstream' EU countries, such as Slovenia and Romania.

APPENDIX – THE DOGS' BIOGS!

After nearly as much research as we put into the caravan, we decided that the Cavapoo was the breed for us. They are small dogs, who combine the intelligence, loyalty and playfulness of the poodle with the affection and calmness of the Cavalier. They don't moult and according to the breeders, "will take as much exercise as you can throw at them."

So here is an introduction to the Fab Four;

Kai – The Lincoln Imp

Our first born; a black and white boy from Laughterton in Lincolnshire. He certainly puts a smile on our faces! Kai is the Hawai'ian word for the ocean, eminently suitable as a canine companion for compulsive, obsessive windsurfers. Kai is a thinker; a sweet and sensitive boy. We maintain that he is not a dog, he is human. This gives him the perfect personality for his voluntary role as a Caring Canine when we are not touring. He brings puppy love to the residents of a Care Home. His gentle nature showed early. When we were comforting a friend who was upset, Kai spontaneously went to the kitchen to collect a little heart-shaped biscuit, which he then pushed carefully on to her thigh while looking tenderly up at her. There was not a dry eye in the house! Kai's coat is that of a tyke and he is prone to spectacular bed-head. Not surprising as he loves his bed and is a bit of a grumblebum in the morning, or in fact, anytime that you wake him up. He approaches each new day with the bewildered look of an earthquake victim being pulled from the rubble. All that is missing is the brick dust in his coat. Kai definitely embodies the saying that you should let sleeping dogs lie.

Rosie – Our Little Chorley Cake

Rosie, our black and white girl, epitomises the spirit of The Boddington's Girl or Cheryl Cole. Beautiful, intelligent, but very much in touch with her Northern roots. She can burp and snore with the best of them and is a cool surf dog, always up for new experiences. She was named partly for the red rose of Lancashire, her (and my) home county and partly for the AC/DC song 'Whole Lotta Rosie' for her size and personality. We thought she was a bit of a porker when we got her, but realised that we were doing her a disservice, since she was crossed with a miniature poodle, rather than a toy poodle like the others. She is not averse to real ale, but her favourite drinks are wine, champagne* and muddy puddle water. She is full of exuberance and will do anything for a treat. If she escapes, which she does frequently because she is "Nosy Rosie" and has to get into EVERY-THING, she answers to "Rosie", "Rosie Poo" or even just "Poo". But only when it suits her!

I stress that we do not give alcohol to Rosie; alcohol is poisonous to dogs, but she sees it as fair game to help herself to an unguarded glass, flute or tankard!

Princess Ruby

We were getting two puppies to keep each other company. Well, the breeder in Chorley had a litter of red puppies and Mark fell in love. "Three dogs is madness!" I maintained, for approximately two whole days. On the third day, I awoke enlightened and decreed that we should get the red puppy. "If you have one dog, you have a commitment. Two dogs, three dogs, what's the difference?" I rationalised. And she was ever so cute. And Mark's Mum, Ruby Joyce, very kindly said that if we wanted her, she would buy the puppy for us. So Mark drove to Chorley and back for the second time in a week and Beautiful Princess Ruby Booby came into our lives.

Ruby is our angel of the morning. She greets each new day with a vigorously wagging tail, a cheery song and the best hugs. She is a happy soul, who even wags her tail in her sleep! She is a proper Princess. She would definitely detect a pea under at least twenty mattresses; she squeals and jumps up frantically to demand the immediate removal of the tiniest of leaves or invisible blades of grass which may have touched her fur. She never comes to get her own treat, knowing that good things come to she who waits. She just about tolerates the fact that the treats are not presented on a silver platter. Her job is running around and sniffing the shoreline, chasing tiny sand flies. She takes it very seriously. Do anything she doesn't like and she wanders off in a huff, particularly if you try and groom her or trim her nails, but she gets lonely quite quickly. She sits to attention, looks you straight in the eye and issues a short, sharp "buff" to let you know that she is ready for you to go over, collect her and lavish her with love!

Lovely Licky Lani Lulu

With three dogs, I was now well on the way to becoming that mad old woman in a dressing gown with about fifty dogs. (I have it on good authority that when women of a certain age start to collect dogs, it is actually a recognised medical condition known as the "Many Paws".)

I knew the fourth pup was inevitable because Mark was still looking at puppies on the internet. By now, I had no objection to adding to the pack. Three just didn't seem like the right number anyway. We decided that we needed one for each hand. Mark drove to Bury St Edmunds to bring back a small, black bundle of fluff with a little white chin. He rang several times on the way home "You know how cute she looked in the pictures? She is even MORE cute than that!"

As soon as we met, she crawled straight onto my lap, licked my nose and curled up. It was love and we called her Lani, the Hawai'ian word for "heaven" or "the sky." Despite her "butter wouldn't melt" looks, Lani is a minx! Had we known her better, we could easily have named her "Gnasher"! She LOVES Rosie, dangling off Rosie's beard and assaulting her regularly with the bionic tongue, much to Rosie's mild annoyance. (Mild annoyance is as cross as Rosie ever gets.) Lani deploys frequent stealth attacks on Ruby, even while Ruby is really busy doing her job and if you're ever looking for that pair of socks or your undies, Lani will be diligently shredding them for you. She instinctively KNOWS that humans prefer lots of fang holes in their pants.

Lani is a pocket rocket who never tires. She goes everywhere at full throttle like Billy Whizz and while the other pups sleep, she remains wide awake and constantly monitors what is going on through the windows. She is prone to long-term disappearing acts in search of ducks or squirrels;

it is all about the thrill of the chase. She is a roller, so however often we wash her, my dog halo (she sleeps on my pillow, curled around my head) is frequently suffused with a faint aura of dung. She pretends that she is not very bright to get away with stuff, but has a few tricks up her sleeve. For example, she knows that a quick bark from a distance gets everyone off the sofa so that she can wander back at leisure to pick her preferred spot. She has recently transferred this skill to the manipulation of humans. She scratches at the door, pretending that she needs to go out in the middle of the night. When I blearily switch on the light and start to dress, she is straight back on the bed and curled up tight, right in the middle of my pillow!

François, whom we met in Penthièvre had Lani taped. She observed that of the four, Lani is "La plus terrible!"

ACKNOWLEDGEMENTS

I would like to thank the following people who have been most instrumental in my journey into authorship and publishing.

Tim Guyse-Williams – for sharing with me the most critical thing about writing – "The most important thing is just to start."

Nicola James – for her unwavering confidence in my writing ability and constant encouragement to publish my work.

Sophie Wallace – author of the excellent "Deerhound Rhodry" books, who has patiently proof-read and edited my prose, put up with my impatient timescales and been a mine of helpful information about the publishing process.

Debbie Purse – at Book Covers for You for her enthusiasm, commitment and for her wonderful cover concepts, which brought to life exactly what was in my head!

Simon Pollock and Spice UK – responsible for that fateful trip down the Zambezi – and for seating me next to Mark at a late New Year Dinner because you thought that we'd get on...

Helen & Bernie – for remaining friends with us, even when we bought a caravan - and for always being there, even during the dark and difficult times surrounding our exit from the corporate world.

Steve – for all the fun and practical advice - as well as making us go to the Motorhome and Caravan Show in the first place!

Ant Kath – for just loving us all!

To My Readers Around the World - to all the wonderful people who follow my blog, www.worldwidewalkies.com and those of you who have bought this book. THANK YOU! Your support means everything.

And of course, Mark, Kai, Rosie, Ruby and Lani - for being my joy, my inspiration and my constant companions!

Dog Bless You All!

ABOUT THE AUTHOR

Jackie Lambert has long had a passion for travel and adventure. Always a bit of a tomboy, it was an accidental white water rafting trip down the Zambezi that really opened her eyes to the experiences that the world has to offer. The trip was not, as she expected, 'floating down the river looking at wildlife.' Somewhere between the adrenaline of tackling Grade 5 rapids in crocodile infested waters and the raw beauty of sleeping under the stars on the banks of the river, she determined that she was no longer content to live her life in thin slices.

Since then, she has travelled as much as time and budget would allow and has rafted major rivers on every continent except Antarctica. Before meeting her husband, Mark, she took a sabbatical from work (although she was single at the time, she asked for - and was granted - "maternity leave"!) to spend several months backpacking around Fiji, Australia and New Zealand.

A keen skier and windsurfer, Jackie is a Team Rider for the UK's National Watersports Festival, to which she has contributed many articles and blogs about windsurfing. She is also the wordsmith behind her own dog-centric caravan travel blog, World Wide Walkies, which has been featured in the Eurotunnel Le Shuttle Newsletter and Dog Friendly Magazine.

She and Mark were made redundant in 2016 – and have been travelling ever since!

Printed in Great Britain
by Amazon

49283614R00118